RED ROSE

To live a life is not as easy as crossing a field.

(old Russian proverb)

RED ROSE

MARGOT TRACEY

DAVID & CHARLES

NEWTON ABBOT   LONDON   NORTH POMFRET (VT)   VANCOUVER

British Library Cataloguing in Publication Data

Tracey, Margot
    Red rose.
    1. Russia – Social life and customs – 1917–
    I. Title
    947.084′1′0924   DK265

    ISBN 0–7153–7440–0

Printed in Great Britain by
Latimer Trend & Company Ltd Plymouth
for David & Charles (Publishers) Limited
Brunel House   Newton Abbot   Devon

Published in the United States of America
by David & Charles Inc
North Pomfret   Vermont 05053   USA

Published in Canada
by Douglas David & Charles Limited
1875 Welch Street   North Vancouver   BC

CONTENTS

INTRODUCTION 7

PART ONE
BORN IN RUSSIA 9

PART TWO
A TOURIST IN RUSSIA 133

INTRODUCTION

Perhaps because the enchantment of my early days in Russia had never quite faded from my memory, I was completely shattered by my first glimpse of Moscow which had once been my home. A Moscow transformed beyond all recognition by the tearing down of old familiar landmarks and churches, the almost pathological renaming of streets, the stretches of ugly apartment blocks, brought me nothing but acute pain and overwhelming sadness. All direct links with the past had gone and, with it, something fine and splendid.

As I speak the language, Russians often mistook me for one of themselves and so, on subsequent visits, I was able to see and hear what an ordinary tourist could never perceive and thus realize the extent to which these wretched people—prisoners in their own land—are muzzled by the absolute power of their bureaucratic rulers.

The constant fear, and the complexity and secrecy of private lives is almost impossible for a free person to understand. In these reminiscences I have invented nothing, but, conscious of so many dangers, I no longer see people I knew and so do not now have the same heart-aches. Also, for obvious reasons, I have concealed identities and altered names and places. It is better that way.

Part One

BORN IN RUSSIA

CHAPTER ONE

'When Papa and Mama were in prison, my sister and I had three soldiers to guard us day and night and anyone who came to see us was arrested as well!'

A teenager at a convent school in Italy, I proudly boasted to young companions curious to find out all about the new girl in their midst. The Russian Revolution of 1917 had thrown me at a tender age into a precarious and frightening world which I had faced with a child's special sense of adaptation and adventure. Very quickly the new sordid existence became the prolongation of a previous disciplined life and I promptly acquired the mistaken idea that only decent people of a certain standing ever went to prison. Now, in unfamiliar surroundings, I only wanted everyone to know my parents had been important people—while my schoolmates, I suspect, probably thought I was the daughter of some criminals. Nevertheless they enjoyed the novelty of my stories, listened to my tales of torment with disbelief and wonder and invariably begged me for more. To them it was like playing 'cops and robbers'. Children, given a chance, are exhibitionists and I was no exception. Conscious of my new popularity, I told them of search-parties coming in the night, of soldiery in dirty boots ripping upholstery with bayonets, of others wiping their filthy hands on brocade curtains and spitting on the shiny parquet floors.

'We had a large, beautiful aquarium in the winter garden,' I would say, 'which Papa had purchased at an exhibition. It had been intended for Alexander III and had his crown and initials encrusted in semi-precious stones among the different seashells from which it was made. A search-party came, one of the soldiers kicked the crown with his boot and it was shattered to pieces.'

I could see the expressions on the faces of my audience as I related the well-remembered episode. They were impressed and I was jubilant. 'One night they came for my papa and took him away,' I would continue, in full swing now. 'They kept him a year in prison as a French hostage and he was only re-united with us on the Finnish frontier.'

'And your mama, tell us what happened to your mama?'

'Oh, my mama,' I would reply, trying to appear casual. 'She just went off one afternoon to visit her dressmaker and did not come back. That's when the soldiers came to guard us. When, after a few days they left, my sister and I stayed quite alone, in a cold, damp cellar and we had nothing to eat!'

'What did you do then?', they begged excitedly. 'Tell us what you did then!'

At some length I would explain the various intricacies of our precarious existence, embellishing where I could but in the main keeping to facts, facts that were completely outside the comprehension of normally brought-up children in the West. Who had ever heard that you could be hungry enough to eat a cat or a dog and be thankful for it? In 1921 refugees like us were as yet an unknown factor and I was the first such child my young companions had ever encountered. So they listened open-mouthed and asked for more stories. If I was in the mood, I would condescend to give them some lurid details and, in particular, a story that troubled me for many years. One of the soldiers who had guarded us had confided that his little girl, the same age as I was, in some remote village from whence he came, had been killed by a horde of roaming hooligans, cut up into pieces and thrown into a cesspool. I reminded him of his child and he assured me I had nothing to fear from him, but the story kept me awake at night for many months. Now, feeling safe at my convent school and insulated by kind nuns against ugly realities, it became my *pièce de résistance*. About the fear I had experienced and the cold and hunger from which I had suffered so cruelly, I kept silent. The last thing I wanted was for anyone to pity me!

My horrific tales soon reached the ears of Mother Superior, a kindly, saintly woman. I was summoned into her presence and she gently, tactfully explained that she knew my stories were quite true, but would I please stop telling them to my little friends?

'You see, they cannot really understand,' she had said.

She must have known that the terrifying mysteries of life which parents are reluctant to reveal to their children were no longer a secret to me and that the revolution had, in a way, robbed me of my childhood. Although I took her advice reluctantly, thereafter I kept my memories to myself and, with a certain sense of superiority, thought my young playmates were just 'babes in the wood'.

At the beginning of the century foreigners in Russia who had established themselves and founded large industries formed almost a separate, proverbially conservative class, and had become the new aristocracy of wealth. They were closely united and many of them had intermarried, thus strengthening their positions. Many more were so Russified that even their foreign names in their Russian guise were unrecognisable. They played a large part in the development of a country where the improvements of civilisation had been notably slow to arrive. Tartar rule had left a deep impression on Russia. For foreigners, it was a patriarchal land of plenty and of oriental hospitality; they thought it was the finest life in the world! Many a simple man rose to the highest post from humble beginnings and was given the status of a 'gentleman' so that his descendants became gentry too.

Such a man was my paternal grandfather, Claude Giraud. He was born in 1836 in the small town of Tarare, some forty kilometres to the north of Lyon in France. Louis XI had introduced silk manufacture into France in 1467 and Louis XIV's Minister, Colbert, introduced in 1667 the manufacture of fine brocades which had previously come from Flanders. In a few years, the industry was well established at Lyon and St Maur. In all probability it was as an apprentice at Lyon that my grandfather learned the different skills which were to serve him so well in Russia, where he went sometime in 1860, one of the many immigrants who were to attempt to organise Russia's large supply of cheap labour, found industries and otherwise help to lessen the gap between Russia and those nations which had already experienced an industrial revolution. Russian agents had been sent to the more advanced industrial countries on recruiting expeditions, and one of these, a rich merchant by the name of Istomine, had met my grandfather in a café in Lyon and persuaded him to come to Russia under contract. In Moscow, Istomine introduced him to a brother-in-law, Kakouchkine, one of whose daughters my grandfather eventually married. They had six children, three boys and three girls. The youngest, Andrew, was my father.

13

Grandfather continued to work for Istomine and it was not until 1868 that he decided to set up on his own. He acquired two handlooms and, with the help of his wife, began to manufacture silk at home. It must have been hard going, but he saw what opportunities awaited him and returned briefly to France to raise some capital. In 1875 he was able to open his own factory with 250 workers installed in unsuitable buildings on rented land. He was a visionary with big ideas; he realised there was bound to be industrial expansion in Russia and was determined that his silk factory would be part of it. He foresaw that the future lay not only in the production of luxury goods for a privileged class but also in the output of cheaper articles within the reach of a larger section of the Russian population. This meant mechanisation, which was unpopular with a workforce fearing for their jobs; nor was it too well received by his clients. Grandfather overcame all these objections and acquired a large new site on the Moskva river with plenty of room for subsequent enlargement. He designed many of his machines, introduced electricity throughout the factory—the first time it had been used on such a scale in Russia—and started what really amounted to a welfare service.

The technical personnel were French or German. They and their families, if they accompanied them, were extremely well looked after, living rent-free in houses or flats and paying nothing for food, lighting or heating. The senior Russian staff were provided for in much the same way. Amenities included lawn tennis, a bowling alley, a billiard room, a meeting hall and a theatre where productions were put on in French and Russian with the participation of the factory's own orchestra.

By 1900, this enterprise had grown into the biggest of its kind in Europe, employing 4,150 workers, rising to 10,000 by 1914. All were accommodated in very large dormitories heated by steam and lit by electricity. They ate in huge dining-rooms which could deal with 4,000 people at a sitting. Each worker received 300 grammes of meat a day. They were also supplied with considerable quantities of *kwass*, a mild Russian beer, and sterilised water for their innumerable cups of tea. The beer was brewed in huge vats on the spot and the workers got through an incredible 20,000 litres of boiling water for their tea each day. On Sundays, and on the holidays of which there were so many in the Russian calendar, the dining-hall was used for lectures, magic-lantern shows and concerts with the orchestra accompanying male and female choirs. There was a large, well-stocked library for those who could read and a hospital and pharmacy run by a doctor and his assistants where treatment and medicine were available. There was a crèche for the very young children of working mothers, and a midwife was in constant attendance. The factory had its own security and safety arrangements as well as its almshouse, and all this was free to the employees and their dependants.

This sort of care for the workers was far in advance of its time in Russia, as in most countries. Even Lenin, in one of his books, paid tribute to it. A parallel can perhaps be found in the paternalism of the great Japanese industrialists between the first and second world wars.

As usual in success stories of this kind, Grandfather had become a millionaire through a combination of hard work, a progressive attitude of mind and favourable circumstances. A disease affecting silkworms hit the French silk industry at about this time and led to greatly reduced production, while a prohibitive tariff on the import of foreign silk was imposed by the Russian authorities in 1893, thus encouraging the domestic industry. So now the products of the factory were sold in every corner of the enormous country. There were showrooms in the heart of Moscow where wholesale orders were dealt with, in the store now known as *Gum* on Red Square, as well as in other big cities.

In 1897 Grandfather received the *Légion d'Honneur* from the French and the Order of St Stanislas from the Russians. His enormous factory exhibited its achievements at the *Exposition Universelle de Paris* in 1900.

Shortly after, a multi-millionaire by now, he retired to his château in Savoy, leaving his business to his three sons. The three daughters received substantial dowries, married Frenchmen and all but one, Aunt Guite, went to live abroad. The factory continued to be administered by my two uncles and my father on the lines grandfather had set. It was built on such solid foundations that there was a saying that the Bank of France might collapse, but never the fortunes of the family.

Our house in Moscow stood in a courtyard surrounded by the red brick buildings of the factory. It backed on to large gardens and, across them, faced the houses of my uncles. Huge iron gates, with a *dvornik* always in attendance to swing them open at any time of day or night for carriages and cars, guarded the entrance to our self-contained fortress within the town and shut us off from all intrusion.

In this very private world I and my numerous cousins spent our early childhood, among the people we loved. We grew up as one large family, strictly controlled by a multitude of nannies, governesses and tutors, not to mention the servants and the workers who all considered themselves part of it and knew us all by name.

The youngest of four children, my birth in 1907 was not particularly welcome as my parents did not want another child. So I was given into the care of Hanochka, a governess who had joined my parents' household on their marriage. She accustomed me from my earliest days to strict discipline and, although I did not know it then, she exemplified the widest tolerance and understanding of others. Although I had other governesses for the different languages I had to learn, my ultimate authority was Hanochka. I was deeply attached to her and thought she would, like the sun and the rain, always be with me. As for my parents, whom I rarely saw, I was allowed to worship them only from afar. They seldom appeared in my small world and I certainly knew nothing of theirs. When, on rare occasions, one of them happened to enter my nursery, the joy of that visit burst upon me like a spring morning.

My two elder brothers lived with tutors in a different part of the house. My sister, Tousia, four years my senior, also preferred other company to mine. The older children often excluded me from their games. 'We can't play with you,' they would say. 'You are much too small and too silly.'

'When will I grow up and become clever?', I would ask Hanochka mournfully, but she invariably failed to give me a satisfactory answer. Instead, she sometimes allowed me to play with Shourka, the daughter of Nadejda the dressmaker and granddaughter of our cook Kirianovna. Sometimes a young relation of Fräulein appeared from somewhere to speak only German. Except for a very occasional sortie with one of my parents and, once a week, opera or ballet, which from the age of six was included in my educational curriculum (through which performances Papa usually slept at the back of the box) my early days in Moscow followed each other with the monotonous regularity of a well oiled clock. The outside world seemed totally inaccessible.

Mama belonged to the impoverished Russian nobility of Austro-German origin. An ancestor of hers had come to Russia as doctor of Catherine II and had eventually been granted by her his patent of nobility. Members of Mama's family had always belonged to the professional classes and stood for liberalism and reform. They were not wealthy. Professional etiquette, for instance, forbade a Russian doctor naming his fee or sending his bill, so most of his patients never paid! Her father was in charge of the huge Foundlings' Hospital on the banks of the Moskva river. A dedicated man fully absorbed by his work, his life was devoted to abandoned children brought to him in large numbers swathed in shawls or laid in wicker baskets and simply deposited on the steps of his hospital or home. His first wife died, leaving him with a girl and a boy. He re-married, but his second wife did not take kindly to her little step-daughter and Mama was sent to one of those institutions where young ladies of the nobility were taught all the graces which were later to adorn their households. She remained there until she was eighteen, returning on the death of her step-mother to look after her father. Barely fifty, he had worn himself out furthering the welfare of his waifs. He had a severe heart condition and knew his days were numbered. There was no money to leave his children and, not unnaturally, he was anxious that his daughter should marry a wealthy man and thus assure her own future as well as that of her young brother, Kostia, to whom she could then act as mother.

In those days in Russia marriages were by arrangement. There was a saying that 'love will follow marriage' and, in a number of cases, it probably did. The innermost feelings of youngsters were rarely consulted but searching inquiries were undertaken into the prospects and backgrounds of both bride and groom. Very soon matrimonial intermediaries became aware that there was a bride on the marriage market, beautiful, accomplished and of noble birth. It was not long before this information reached my French grandfather who was looking for a suitable wife for his youngest son. Eventually, he called on my maternal grandfather to ask for her hand in marriage. Mama at nineteen already possessed more than the prettiness of youth. Her features were regular, her grey-green eyes were fine with an intelligent and pleasing frankness of expression. She had a beautiful complexion, a great deal of dignity and walked with the stateliness of a queen. A glow of indefinable radiance shone in her eyes and she was one of those rare beings whom people instinctively love. Quite clearly here was a girl of character and spirit who would represent well the fortune he had amassed. My grandfather was impressed. Because Mama was slim, she always said it had been lucky for her my grandfather was French. Had he been Russian, her chances of being approved would have largely depended on her weight and stoutness. A thin girl was considered a bad business advertisement!

Mama, in later years, often said how generous and kind her future father-in-law had been to her that day.

'My wife and I will shortly be retiring to France and you and my son will then have our house,' he had said, and mentioned the income he proposed to give the young couple.

'Will it be sufficient? Will you be able to manage?' he had asked with great solicitude.

Mama, who had never handled so much money, thought it was to be a yearly allowance and quite adequate.

'Oh, yes,' she had replied politely, 'it is most generous of you.'

But the sum mentioned was a monthly one and it made her rich beyond all her expectations, and she was able to send her brother to university. She took to her new position like a fish to water and thereafter would always enjoy money more than Papa, whose French blood sometimes inclined him to put on the brakes.

At first, it seems, my parents' marriage was happy. They entertained lavishly, put on plays and concerts in their private theatre and shared a love of horses. Soon the stables were filled with thoroughbreds which they tried to conceal when my French grandparents came on their yearly visits from France. All the grooms were then mobilised to walk the animals in the adjoining fields, leaving only a few in the stables in case Grandpa ventured there. Somehow they were ashamed to admit to him the extent of their extravagance.

I do not know when Papa and Mama started to drift apart as they never quarrelled in public. They were complete opposites in every way and, in the exalted positions they occupied, there must have been plenty of opportunities for flirtations and temptations. Once, looking for Hanochka, I inadvertently burst into Mama's apartments. The scene that confronted me is still fresh in my mind. Mother was in her coat and hat as if ready to go somewhere and she was crying. I heard Hanochka say:

'You cannot, you must not do it. You have four children and you will regret it.'

Then they saw me.

'What is it Margocha?', Hanochka asked, trying to look as if nothing was amiss while Mama smiled at me through tear-stained eyes.

'I have finished my lessons,' I stammered lamely, but for days I wondered why my beautiful mama had been so upset.

Much later I would discover that Papa was a good man but not easy to live with. Born wealthy, he considered himself an important person. Charming with strangers, he reserved his bad moods for home consumption. Mama was headstrong and *avant garde*. She did not disguise her contempt for some of Papa's relatives whom she considered middle class, narrow minded and *nouveaux riches*. It was an open secret that she had committed a *mésalliance* by marrying into trade. She had done it to re-assure her ailing father but some of her family had cut her because of it. So after her father's death she drew closer to her brother; they were deeply devoted to each other and had their own circle of Russian friends. Mama was determined to lead her own life the way she chose. In 1904, flouting all conventions, she travelled alone to Egypt, at a time when no lady in Moscow was expected to walk out unaccompanied. She remained indifferent to gossip and to Papa's outcry, so, in order to make her toe the line, he cut off her supply of money. Mama was in Cairo at the time. Annoyed, she found herself a rich admirer and did not return to Moscow a day earlier than planned.

At no time in childhood did I suspect that all was not well between my parents and for this I shall always be grateful. 'Not in front of the children' was a motto to which all grown-ups in our household strictly adhered. So when Papa sulked for days and walked about like a black cloud, morose and silent, I only wondered. No other female member of the family possessed Mama's independent spirit and true, unreflective courage. Although they all envied her, they were much too conventional to emulate her. But how often, in years to come, would I hear relatives speak with admiration of her because, never petty or

19

timid, she was the only one to have enjoyed the money and position to the hilt while the going was good!

At an early age I became aware that I never went anywhere with both my parents. To go with Papa meant an open carriage or car which he usually drove himself. Mama had a Swiss chauffeur and a closed car which always made me feel sick. Yet I preferred being with her. Her presence alone held such glamour that it transcended everything else. No wonder she was called the Queen of Moscow! Besides, I dreaded Papa's invitations, for if I was only to mention asking Hanochka's permission he invariably became annoyed. 'She's only your governess, darling—you don't have to ask her.'

This to me made no sense at all. Hanochka was all-important and I felt hurt that she meant nothing to Papa. So feeling guilty and resentful, I had to go without her authorisation. Yet, if she reproached me on my return, I would rather have died than repeat Papa's humiliating words. No wonder then that whatever he bought me on those rare jaunts was never right. He was supposed to spoil me, but I did not want the French porcelain doll the salesman brought out, rubbing his hands and telling Papa how wonderful it was. A humble rag doll would have been a greater success because, not understanding money values, I only longed to be like other children. So I would wait impatiently for the time when I could smash the silly face on the parquet floor of my nursery and pretend it was an accident. How many precious dolls I smashed that way, I do not remember, but there must have been quite a few. I always behaved badly when hurt and, unconsciously, I was avenging what I considered an insult to Hanochka.

Years later, of course, I understood Papa's motives. He wanted it said that he never refused his little daughter anything. Poor Papa, he meant well and I grew to love him when he became a poor and profoundly humble man.

There were never such problems with Mama.

'Run along and ask Hanochka's permission to come shopping with me,' she would gaily say and, hand in hand, we would depart and she would buy me what I wanted and only laugh when I chose some unexpected horror. How proud I was of her when people stared, how I wished I could be with her more often! Secretly I longed for some sort of serious illness, anticipating all sorts of delights from such an eventuality. Once, with a very virulent form of influenza, I had been moved into Mama's bedroom and slept in Papa's place while he was relegated to his dressing-room. I could sniff her pillows from which rose the faint and familiar perfume of Houbigant's *Quelques Fleurs* which, from then on, I would always associate with her and recognise anywhere. My illness had been such bliss, I hoped with all my heart the experience could be repeated. My mother was an unattainable divinity and I worshipped her, but it was to Hanochka that I felt close.

CHAPTER TWO

Uncle Paul, my father's brother, was the financial head of the family and my favourite uncle. His features were rather blunt and his hair receded but his fine, merry eyes always twinkled and there was a feeling of gaiety whenever he was around. A born optimist, he had a way with him and people could not help liking him; with more money than he knew what to do with, he indulged in the pleasure of spoiling those he loved. He had married very young and his wife, Aunt Isabelle, had been an eminently suitable match because she was the daughter of another French industrialist. Furthermore, her brother, Uncle Sacha, who was also my godfather, had married his and Papa's youngest sister, Aunt Guite.

When Aunt Isabelle dolled herself up, she could look quite attractive but she was the sort of woman one did not notice. Narrow-minded and boring, nothing ever seemed to disturb her self-satisfied placidity. Besides, she had no vitality and her husband was bursting with it. After the first few years of their marriage it must have become apparent they had not much in common and so they imperceptibly found themselves going their own different ways, with no scenes and no quarrels. In fact, because of the childhood and family ties which bound them firmly together, they always remained solicitous of each other's welfare.

Of the children born to them only the eldest, Edward, had been a boy and he became a very important part of my uncle's existence. Lured by the vision of a son to succeed him, of whom he could be proud, he lavished his affection on the boy until, on his return from a yearly trip abroad, the nineteen-year-old youngster confronted him with the announcement that he had fallen in love with a girl three years his senior, the daughter of one of the factory's washerwomen! She was with child and he intended to marry her when he came of age. There was a terrible scene; both were turned out of the house that very day and sent off to Paris on a one-way ticket. From that moment, the unwritten family law kept everybody silent. No-one spoke of Edward or dared to mention his name. It was as if he had never existed and all photographs of him disappeared from family albums.

Being only four at the time I had, of course, hardly been aware of my cousin's existence or disgrace and would only hear the whole story in all its bitterness when I grew up. Edward had never been very bright. Nor had he, as a rich man's son, been trained for any work. Cruelly exiled without a penny he eked out a miserable existence somewhere in France. My uncle never forgave him although, pathetically, Edward named his two children Paul and Isabelle, in memory of the parents who had so completely renounced him. I never met Edward or his children but an old friend of mine, not so long ago, came across the son, who had become quite an important personage in France. My friend happened to mention me, only to have the subject summarily dismissed.

'I do not wish to know any member of that family,' he had said.

Apparently he too could not forgive.

In 1913 Uncle Paul's eldest daughter Suzy had reached the age of eighteen and my uncle and aunt decided it was time for her to marry. She was a pretty girl and very gentle; it was common knowledge that she would have a large dowry and therefore could make a very brilliant match, but for some reason there were no pretenders—perhaps because the family was emphatic that the future husband had to be a Frenchman.

A survey was therefore made of all the eligible young men they knew in France and the choice fell on the son of an associate and friend of Grandfather with whose family ours was already connected by marriage. He was deemed suitable in every way, rich, brilliant and attractive. An invitation was sent for him to visit Moscow which he accepted with alacrity. He was most anxious to see the Russia which friends and relations found so enthralling. He came in October, was received *en prince* and enjoyed the proverbial Russian hospitality. The best houses were wide open to him, he went bear-hunting with the men, danced with the pretty women at balls given in his honour and rode beautiful thoroughbreds with both. He had a wonderful time but Suzy held no attractions for him and he found her dull. He had no intention of proposing marriage. Why should he? Her wealth did not impress him, he was rich himself, and there were plenty of seductive women throwing themselves at him whom he did not have to marry. After a glorious six weeks he took leave of his disappointed hosts and returned to France as fancy-free as he had come. My uncle and aunt, not unnaturally, considered that their daughter had been slighted and it became more imperative than ever to show this impertinent young pup that Suzy could marry anyone she chose and at any time. More feelers were discreetly put out, and a second invitation followed to another possessor of suitable credentials. Michel Arnoux was a budding young barrister who had graduated with honours and, to acquire financial know-how, now worked in a Paris bank. Rumour had it that he was outstandingly good-looking and irresistible to women. What rumour did not add was that he was ambitious and unscrupulous and determined to succeed by any means. When the invitation reached him he already knew all there was to know and was determined not to miss the opportunity of landing such a rich heiress. So he hurried to Moscow where Aunt Isabelle was the first to fall under his spell as he put himself out to charm her. He was attentive, modest, pleasant. The silly woman became his most enthusiastic ally and never realised that Michel had the special gift of being able to sweep women off their feet. A fortnight after his arrival, he formally proposed and was accepted. Suzy and her parents were overjoyed. The wedding was fixed for 16 January at the French Church in Moscow, the reception to be held at our house where the dining-room giving on to the large winter garden could easily accommodate 600 guests. Meantime, Michel returned to Paris to set up house for his bride.

In Moscow the preparations for the festivities started in earnest, with great excitement and jealousies among the servants of both households, who all claimed various honours for themselves. The existing butlers, valets and maids would be insufficient to look after the number of people expected to attend and extra staff had to be engaged. Famous chefs invaded the kitchens, well-known *maîtres d'hôtels* were put in charge of training a battalion of servants, throwing somewhat out of joint the nose of our butler, Sergei Philipoch, whose usual grumblings increased.

'Of course there's no need for any hiring,' he kept muttering as he sat in his office supervising his underlings as they counted the dinner services, silver, glasses, tablecloths, napkins, etc. 'When the President of France dined with us in 1896 there were even more guests and there was still enough of everything.'

To add to my excitement, dressmakers invaded even my nursery. It was the first time I was to attend such a big occasion, and also the last! Sixteen children, of whom I was the youngest, were to sit at a special table under the surveillance of three governesses.

The night before I suffered martyrdom while Hanochka brushed and rolled my long black hair on curlers. The lumps with which my head was eventually covered were as hard as rocks and gave me a sleepless, restless night, but the result after the instruments of torture had been removed was a profusion of long, beautiful curls. Hanochka never stopped telling me that '*pour être belle il faut souffrir*', nor did I escape the countless other recommendations of good behaviour.

On the appointed day, the bride arrived at the church on the arm of her father but the bridegroom, who should have been waiting, for some reason was not there. Something had gone astray. There was a lot of running up and down the aisle, a lot of consultations. Michel had been staying at a near-by hotel. What could have happened? Had there been some kind of accident? The bride, on the verge of tears, must have wondered where her good-looking groom, whom half the female population of the town envied her, had disappeared? Besides, it was humiliating to be kept waiting on her day of days.

Uncle Paul, as usual, took matters into his own hands. Entrusting his daughter to my father, he rushed to the hotel in search of Michel while the gathered assembly wondered, whispered and waited. Forty minutes later both men reappeared, smiling happily. It had all been such a silly mistake! The Beau Michel, as everyone now called him, tired after his stag party the night before, had overslept and the hotel porter had overlooked the instructions to wake him. Profuse excuses were offered all round, Michel kissed his bride and dear Mama-in-law and harmony was restored. This, after all, was Russia, where time did not matter and an hour's difference was a small price to pay for a life of delirious happiness, or so everyone must have thought. . . .

Uncle Paul had found Michel in his hotel in bed with what in those days was so charmingly called 'a cocotte'. Surprised by such impudence, what was my poor uncle to do? His daughter was waiting at the altar for the scoundrel whom he and his wife had welcomed as a son. Suzy had already had a disappointment and people had gossiped. Now, important guests were waiting at the church, a large number had travelled from France especially for the occasion, six hundred of them were expected to lunch! Numerous other festivities were pending and here was Beau Michel caught *in flagrante delicto* by his future father-in-law! Probably there were plenty of skeletons in the family cupboards; the habit of sweeping everything unpleasant under the carpet was very strong in their French blood. Uncle Paul was no exception; if he had been, future tragedies might perhaps have been averted; but he was a proud man and could not face that sort of scandal.

Curtly, he told Michel to hurry as his bride was waiting. God alone knows with what wrath in his heart he stood over him while he dressed, totally ignoring the poor wench who had disappeared into the bathroom, and oblivious of the lame explanations Michel tried to offer. Presently, he walked out of the hotel, as dapper as ever, followed closely by the groom still straightening his tie with trembling hands and reflecting no doubt what a close shave it had been! Entering the church with a gracious smile and with perfect composure, Uncle Paul led his daughter to the altar and gave her away in marriage.

In the household of Uncle Victor, my father's other brother, things ran smoothly. He had married a Frenchwoman from his father's home town. Aunt Frances seemed to perpetually wear mourning for some deceased distant relative as was the custom then in France, and, as a very good Catholic, produced a child every year. I was told she had had fourteen in all, but by the time I came on the scene only seven had survived, mostly boys. My aunt hated life in Russia and all things Russian. She neither could nor would speak the language; it was the Frenchest of all French homes and even the children's nannies were French. As for my cousins, as soon as they were old enough, they were despatched to schools in France and only came back for holidays. Therefore, it was not surprising that with the outbreak of first the war and then the revolution, the excuse to leave was promptly taken.

CHAPTER THREE

I vividly remember the summer of 1914 and the day war was declared, because that evening the usual firework display in honour of my birthday was cancelled. We were on our estate in Himki. To reach it, you travelled twenty-five kilometres on the St Petersburg Chaussée until you came to a tiny village, appropriately named 'Mare's Puddle', where large ruts of muddy, stagnant water in the unpaved clay road made it precarious for any transport. Here you turned right and joined a private road which twisted and turned for three kilometres until suddenly you came upon a large, wooden *dacha*, all fretwork and pink paint, standing peacefully on a hillock among the birches, overlooking ornamental gardens that rolled down smoothly to the green fringes of a lake which prisoners had dug out of swamps during the Russo–Japanese war. The lake was enormous and mysterious, in parts very deep. Wooden bridges crossed it at various points. On it were several islands and a quantity of boats to take us to and fro. On the islands white rabbits bred and, on the banks, basking in the sun, large and small green frogs continually plopped into the water as I tried to catch them. Multicoloured dragonflies, sparkling like precious jewels, darted all around chasing small insects, while the water itself teemed with fish. The profusion of life here filled me with wonder and delight and I wished the days would never end. As soon as winter snows began to melt and the ice broke on the Moskva river, the rooks returned to build their nests in the garden and I started counting the days to 15 May when the summer holidays began.

On the eve of that day, cartloads of luggage left Moscow for Himki, ambling past sleepy villages and heralding our arrival as fair-haired children ran around them with cries of joy. Next day, we ourselves travelled by train or car and were hardly in the house before one of the maids would announce: '*Barinia*, there's a delegation from Marfouchino to welcome you.' Barefooted

27

peasants from surrounding villages flocked to the estate with greetings and blessings, bringing bunches of spring flowers and lilies of the valley and being rewarded with pails of vodka for the men and money for the women. The same scene was re-enacted in the autumn when we returned to Moscow, except that mushrooms and berries then replaced the flowers.

Soon the sound of horses' hoofs on the cobbled stones of the courtyard brought me running to the front porch. The village 'pope' and his 'deacon' had arrived to bless the house and its inhabitants, the usual practice without which the superstitious Russian servants would have refused to take up residence. The contraption in which the clergy travelled, called a *drojki*, was really nothing more than a long, narrow board on four wheels which the two men, balancing precariously, somehow managed to bestride with their cassocks lifted above their knees. Mama would meet them and lead them into the drawing-room where all the household had already gathered. Both holy men, on entering, bowed deeply and crossed themselves three times in front of the large ikon of Our Lady of Iberia. Then the pope, turning towards the assembly, pronounced the traditional words of welcome while, at a small table covered with a white cloth, a housemaid helped the deacon to arrange the implements of worship. The short service was followed by a procession through the whole house, the *batiushka* intoning the *Gospody pomiloui* (Lord have mercy) to which all replied, and sprinkling with holy water every corner of every room, presumably to cast out the devils. He then took refreshment with us while the deacon was similarly feasted in the kitchens and the scraggy nag which brought them received due attention in the stables. There would be more mumblings and blessings as the visitors prepared to take their leave and pocketed with visible pleasure the gold roubles Mama slipped into their hands.

Most of the summer the house in Himki was full of guests. They came in droves, stayed for weeks and lodged in a special pavilion adjoining the house. Here Mama and Uncle Kostia entertained their Russian friends. Papa, busy at the factory, came down only for long week-ends. Uncle Kostia was a judge and was liable to be recalled to town at short notice, at least that was his excuse for not going to his distant estate with his wife and children, some of whom also came to stay. No doubt he found it more fun to chaperone Mama and her gay friends. A wit and merrymaker called Stepka came for the duration. His rôle was that of a professional jester and he spent his life as guest in rich people's houses. All he required for this parasitic existence was a postal box in Moscow where he collected his never-ending flow of invitations. All summer he was at the beck and call of my parents. A man in his early forties, with a goatee beard, greyish curly hair, always immaculately dressed and groomed, he made everybody laugh, told jokes and animated dinner parties or even capered about imitating some Cossack dancer. He also had to put up with all kinds of horseplay which demanded a considerable amount of *souplesse*. In return for his services, which were peculiar to old Russia and were an established pattern of our life in the country, he was rewarded with an unimaginable degree of comfort and de-luxe living. He was patronised by my parents but despised by Philipoch and the other servants.

'He never tips anyone as he should,' Shourka, my main informant, scornfully complained. This, in a country where everybody was expected to tip, seemed very strange. I do not remember his ever bringing us children or my mother the slightest present. His type of parasite was to vanish completely with the advent of the revolution, but we did hear that for a time Stepka made a good living as a black marketeer.

From morning until nightfall, young girls in the national costumes of some distant province weeded the flower beds and the paths on the estate, their picturesque dresses and gay kerchiefs blending into the greenery as they went about their work. Every summer, at our bailiff's request to a village elder, about fifty such 'weeders' came to us under the supervision of an old dragon of a peasant woman called Mamka. The girls lived somewhere in the grounds and were a jolly lot who also helped with haymaking and fruit picking. I always knew when it was time to gather the luscious, ripe strawberries and raspberries which grew in profusion at the bottom of the orchard, as continual singing would then come from that direction. 'So long as they sing, the fruit is being gathered and not eaten,' Mamka used to say.

Some of the girls came year after year and I knew them by name. On warm evenings their voices and laughter drifted towards the house, across the lake. On special occasions, to the accompaniment of a village lad's harmonica, they entertained my parents and their guests with singing and dancing, for which they received extra payment. All the time the old Mamka watched. The girls in her care were all young virgins and it was her responsibility to see they returned to their villages as virgins, and with their dowries suitably augmented.

Festivities in Himki must have continually succeeded each other but, being only a child, I witnessed the dazzling splendours and the bustle from afar. Sent to bed at 8pm, I would listen to music coming from the gardens where, on hot nights, an orchestra played and dinner parties took place. Through my open bedroom window, as I fell asleep, I breathed the soft air flooded with the fragrance of acacias and lime trees in blossom. In the mornings, carriages and horses often waited in the courtyard and I was sometimes allowed to join an expedition, riding my pony, which was often unreliable and headstrong. It would gallop away merrily and suddenly stop, lowering its head in front of a ditch, with the obvious result. So Mama preferred me to take a seat in one of the carriages. She was much more relaxed and accessible to me here. Also, so long as I occupied myself and did not just sit gazing into space, I was free to roam and was not made to copy lines or darn a sock—Hanochka's usual remedy for idleness.

Under Mama's bedroom windows grew heliotropes and sweet peas and I always imagined this was the reason Mama's perfume was called *Quelques Fleurs*. If Hanochka was not about, I strolled in the direction of the forbidden kitchens where Kirianovna the cook often handed me some succulent tit-bit or where I could perhaps have a few words with Shourka, to play with whom I had first to obtain Hanochka's permission. The adjoining woods behind the house were full of wild flowers and berries which I liked to pick, but fear of imaginary wolves made me afraid to stray too far and I preferred to gather the dancing cornflowers in the nearby golden fields.

Trinity Sunday was a special feast when young peasant girls from distant villages came dressed in their finery, carrying according to custom a small colourfully decorated birch tree. Around this they circled hand in hand under our windows to the accompaniment of popular songs. I was allowed to join in these celebrations and sang and danced with them. They were invited to return in June for Tousia's birthday, and did so accompanied by many others.

A long table in the garden was covered with a bright tablecloth. On it stood an enormous brass samovar brought from the kitchens and polished to look like gold, surrounded with cups and saucers and a profusion of national delicacies, honey, spicy cakes, cracknels, fudge, jams and sweetmeats. The guests arrived barefoot, their *laptis* (shoes made of bark) slung over their shoulders but put on when they came in sight of the house. When at our invitation they sat down, Tousia and I helped with the service. The girls were invariably on their best behaviour, awed by the occasion, biting delicately on lumps of sugar and sipping their tea through them in the traditional peasant way. When they had eaten and drunk to their hearts' delight and wiped their mouths with the backs of their hands, in spite of the napkins provided, they would turn their cups upside down and deposit the tiniest bit of sugar on top—the customary way of signifying they had finished. Singing, dancing and merrymaking would then begin, all centred on Tousia, who was the queen of the party. Before the feast ended, from a heap of parcels stacked nearby, she would distribute a present to each girl in turn. Finally, taking off their shoes once more, the merry crowd would disperse and for a long time the girls' voices and laughter would echo over the woods and fields, intermingling with the sound of distant church bells and the lowing of cattle returning of their own accord from pasture.

In the still summer night, with the comforting nightlight burning under the ikon in the corner of my room, I would listen for the first tentative, gentle note of the nightingale which would presently erupt into a resounding song, and I would wonder which one it was. (Some, like real primadonnas, sang much better than others!) Or maybe I would hear Matvei, the coachman, let loose the sixteen hounds that patrolled the estate at night. Whether these dogs ever caught an intruder I do not know, but one morning Lukeria, the poultry woman, burst into the breakfast-room, in tears.

'*Barinia, barinia,*' she cried, almost hysterical. 'There is not a live chicken left. Last night this good-for-nothing Matvei got drunk and the dogs broke into the chicken house and slaughtered the lot.'

After this commotion Matvei was severely reprimanded and swore he would never touch vodka again.

This was the childhood I knew, this large, simple existence

which only varied between the old house in Moscow in the winter and the country estate in summer, those sometimes very hot summers with tropical storms and enchanting, long, leisurely days. It was a peaceful, patriarchal way of life where everyone belonged and which I associated with the Russia I loved. Nothing, I thought, could interrupt it, let alone alter its course.

That particular autumn, probably because of the war mobilisation and the hurried departure of my German Fräulein, Tousia and I were sent back to town by rail, with Niania. She had long been retired but continued to live in the house and, occasionally, was asked to perform some small service. Going by train with her was a very special treat. We could indulge our fancies because, as with all Russian *nianias*, children could do no wrong and she would put up with almost anything. On one occasion—I must have been four years old—Niania complained of a headache. She lay on a couch in my nursery with her eyes closed, moaning gently. Hanochka was not about and I became very concerned and decided to nurse Niania back to health. I had seen grown-ups put a damp cloth on a forehead to ease pain, so I pulled a chair to the large marble washstand, picked up a sponge and tried to turn on the tap. It would not yield and I did not want to disturb the invalid. Moved by the best intentions imaginable, I had an inspiration. I pulled my potty out of the bedside cabinet, sat on it for a moment, then plunged the sponge into it and on to Niania's forehead. As the warm liquid trickled down her face, she put her tongue out and murmured, somewhat surprised.

'Why, it *is* salty!' Then she opened her eyes, understood and started to grumble. I was very annoyed and slightly hurt because, after all, I had only tried to help.

Now, installed in a first-class compartment, I proceeded to read aloud all the *nicht heraus lehnen* signs in various languages and to ask innumerable questions about the passing scenery.

Niania always carried an enormous bundle, tied up peasant fashion at the four corners. She rummaged through it and produced, as if by magic, all sorts of tempting delicacies. Presently she took out a small chamber-pot. In the past it had been indispensable on her travels with us—we were never allowed to use the WC reserved for ordinary mortals, for fear of infection. But then it had been on longer journeys and we had occupied a private compartment. Now we had both outgrown such requisites anyway, and I vaguely wondered what Niania was up to? Suddenly I saw the surprised looks on the faces of the passengers. Niania, it seems, had found a good use for this elegant vessel. She had packed her own lunch into it and, quite oblivious of the effect created, was now heartily tucking into it.

A small room next to the attic in our Moscow house, more of a closet really as it had no window, was solidly padlocked most of the time. Here were stored the presents my godfather, Uncle Sacha, gave me four times a year, for my birthday, my nameday, Christmas and Easter. As an occasional treat Hanochka sometimes displayed these to me and, according to her, I was to have them when I came of age as they were of great value and not intended for a child. They all possessed a quality of mystery and probably because of that I still remember some of them, particularly the tiny enamel Easter eggs and amusing animals from Fabergé, to which shop I often went with Papa. Others, such as canteens of silver and various *objets d'art*, I was unable to appreciate.

Uncle Sacha was a third-generation Frenchman settled in Russia and his name was well known throughout the country from the soaps, powders, perfumes and toiletries of all sorts which carried it on their labels. His great-grandfather, a chemist, had run a small perfume shop on the Champs Élysées in Paris in the 1820s. It became so successful that he decided to try his luck in the new world and, taking his two young sons, went to Philadelphia. Maybe he was a restless soul or maybe he did not like America for after two years, hearing that a lot of French capital was being invested in Russia, he decided to go there and see for himself. Caught by the spell of Moscow, he also found that in the field of perfumery there was no competition whatsoever and he could easily make a fortune. He instructed his two sons to liquidate the American business and join him in Moscow, despite the fact that the talented boys, aged only sixteen and fourteen at the time, had made an unqualified success of the business during their father's absence! On their arrival in Russia the eldest contracted some illness and died. The youngest, Henri, who was to become Uncle Sacha's father, helped to start a small factory, at first mainly for the manufacture of soap at popular prices, so as to reach the masses who at that time were almost unaware of such a commodity. The venture prospered, the old man died and Henri married the daughter of a French tutor who taught children of the Russian nobility and, with her help, built an enormous business which soon rivalled the large perfumeries of France.

Henri's interests lay in many directions. He had a rare feeling for art and was a compulsive collector of antiques. His way of acquiring treasures was, even by the standards of that time, highly original. He would leave his competent wife in charge of the business and the children and travel to France, where he spent his time ferreting in countless antique and junk shops. If his connoisseur's eye detected anything of interest, he would drive a hard bargain for the entire contents of the shop, which were then inventoried, packed, sealed and put into storage. After several such operations, he would charter a special goods train in which these treasures were sent back to Russia where intensive sorting took place, the best, naturally, going to his own collection. Other objects were distributed at random among his relatives or their children and some were given to various charities of which he was a staunch patron. As a result there were quantities of strange antique toys and games in all the family attics, such as I would never see again!

In time Henri became so Russified that he lived and behaved exactly in the manner of a wealthy Russian trader, with all the typical extravagances and autocratic habits, doing as he pleased. Thus, I was to learn, if a joint was not cooked to his satisfaction, he bellowed like a bull and simply flung it out of the nearest window. How his very French wife reacted to such whims I was never told. On his death, his two children inherited the enormous wealth he had accumulated as well as his various collections.

Uncle Sacha did not resemble his father. He had a gentle and retiring disposition and he looked after his wife, Aunt Guite, as if she were a child. Events liable to upset her were hidden from her. Aunt Guite was a tiny brunette with regular features which resembled my father's, but a sallow complexion and the tiniest of waists. She made me somehow think of a wasp, except there was no sting in her. She must have been a hypochrondriac from an early age and she was supposed to suffer from nerves, headaches and other similar ailments. She certainly could induce seizures at will. On the rare occasions when she came to visit, Uncle Sacha kept a close, protective watch over her as she was liable to faint at the slightest provocation, which greatly amused all of us children because we had spotted that when she did, there was always a comfortable sofa or armchair behind her, into which she could pass out gracefully, to be presently revived with smelling salts, always at hand when she was about. We were used to her oddities and, I must confess, rather enjoyed them. In her better moments and in her own house she emerged to play the harp or sit by it in a romantic pose, and there were quantities of photographs about depicting her that way. My two cousins were brought up by governesses—it was said she was too delicate to have the worry of children—and when she occasionally summoned them, she kissed them tenderly and called them 'angels', as she did all of us, because, we suspected, she could not remember our names.

People said Uncle Sacha was a man of duty but surely he was guilty of encouraging her to live in a world completely detached from all reality. It seems incredible, but she was not informed of the 1914 war! Papa had volunteered for a time into the Russian Army and, when that year he returned for Christmas, she happened to see him in uniform at a party in our house. She immediately passed out on the nearest sofa and I can still hear all the relations shaking their heads and murmuring: 'Poor Guite, she's had such a shock. She did not know about the war.' Young as I was, I thought it very strange.

To protect her from such harsh realities, as soon as dark clouds began to gather, Uncle Sacha took her, his family and a fair slice of his fortune out of Russia to France. His wonderful presents to me stopped, although I hardly noticed it. You do not get attached to things you have not really possessed, and anyway I was too young to care. Whether the presents in the closet were eventually absorbed into some museum or whether they were looted, I shall never know. As for his priceless collection of pictures, impossible to move in wartime, they now grace the walls of Russian museums. I still have a catalogue dated 1898, when he exhibited them for charity in Moscow, listing pictures by Guardi, Canaletto, Renoir, Matisse, Monet, Brueghel, Van der Velde, Cuyp, Fragonard, Buchet and Hals, to name only a few.

CHAPTER FOUR

At the beginning of the war hysterical patriotism and hatred of the Germans was rife and the Jews, as usual, were blamed as well. In Himki some German properties had been burned down to the ground. In Moscow too, there were many terrible pogroms and anyone with a German name was liable to be attacked. One afternoon, walking with Hanochka in Kouznetski Most, we heard extraordinary noises and, suddenly, a hundred yards in front of us, a piano landed on the pavement producing a mighty explosion. The shop being attacked was Zimmerman's and the name alone must have attracted the attention of roaming hooligans. With yells of 'Down with Jews, to Hell with Germans!' men armed with axes were hacking at pianos, harps, violins, and drums and pushing them out of windows into the street. As each instrument landed with a terrific cacophony, the noise became deafening and almost supernatural. The intensity of this nightmarish concert was reinforced by screams of joy from the approving populace which now surrounded us on all sides. As Hanochka and I hurried away, the spectacle became even more frightening with the arrival of the fire brigade and the police, and I think my deep-rooted fear of crowds dates from that moment.

In 1915, with the war truly on, father donated a newly built apartment house for use as a hospital for the wounded returning in increasing numbers from the front. Mama and Hanochka put on Red Cross uniforms for work there, and occasionally I would be taken to visit some of the men. Grown-ups talked of unrest, scandals at Court, reverses at the front, but I was still confined to my own world and was diligently preparing my school entry exams.

Some months before, Aunt Isabelle had received word that Suzy was expecting a baby. As the date of the confinement approached, all the household became involved in deciding who should go to France for the occasion.

36

'I cannot let my daughter have her baby without me,' moaned my aunt.

Suzy's Niania, who had brought her up, joined in. '*Barinia*, I am coming with you. The poor *golubka* (little pigeon) will need me.'

'In that case,' my aunt replied, 'the two younger children and their governess had better come too.'

Niania agreed. 'The *barinia* will have to take her maid, Douniacha,' she added.

'Naturally,' said Aunt Isabelle and informed her husband of her decision. Uncle Paul raised no objections.

'Of course we must go, dearest,' he assured his wife. He was determined not to miss the arrival of his first grandchild and, of course, he had to take his valet.

The difficulty of a journey in wartime through Finland, Norway and England, and the expense of travelling with such a retinue, never even entered my uncle's calculations. They spent five weeks in Paris welcoming the new baby before the caravan returned to Moscow. All, that is, except Niania, who chose to remain and bring up the child. She did not trust a French nurse to do so efficiently. Luckily for her, once more no-one protested and so she escaped the horrors of the revolution and ended her life peacefully in France.

It was left to Douniacha, the maid, to tell the servants on her return all the marvellous details about Paris. 'Everyone is so clever there,' she kept repeating. 'Almost as clever as our *barines*. All, but all the servants speak French.'

In 1916 I went to school for the first time, driven there on dark winter mornings and returning home to the purring of the eternal samovar, unchanging symbol of Russian life. On my first day I was surrounded by a number of little girls, examining me like some weird animal and all asking questions.

'Are you very rich? How rich are you, Frenchy?'

'Ah,' one of the little girls emphatically declared, 'she is a very rich French Frog.'

Until then I had never heard any reference to money. I did not know or even suspect that I was a millionaire's daughter nor did I have any idea of my family's importance. We were poor little rich girls, strictly brought up to be grateful for anything. If I wanted sweets, I might be given a few kopeks to buy some, but not always, as we were certainly not indulged in any way. So now all these questions puzzled and embarrassed me as I did not know the answers and could only stammer in reply: 'I don't know, I'll have to ask my governess.'

When I did, Hanochka looked surprised and, for some reason, displeased.

'Why do you want to know?' she asked.

'The girls at school keep asking me.'

She pondered for a few seconds, frowning in a familiar way.

'Tell them you are neither rich nor poor, just . . .' (there was a pause) 'just medium.'

But I was not completely satisfied.

'Hanochka, why did they call me "Frenchy"?'

'Well, you are French because your Papa is.'

'But why "Frog" then?'

'What does it matter, child? I suppose because the French eat frogs; they taste like chicken.'

No, I thought, perhaps it did not matter, but somehow from that very moment I felt a breed apart. My emotional awareness had just begun to stir. I did not foresee how durable that feeling of not belonging would be. 'Frenchy' in Russia, I would become 'Roussky' in France, 'a Parisian' in America and, eventually, 'a foreigner' in England. But that is much later. . . .

Everywhere people were talking about how badly the war was going. Mother and Hanochka spent most of their time at the hospital, which was full to capacity with severely wounded men. More and more I was left to my own devices and the care of whoever happened to be available, but holidays, birthdays and namedays were still suitably observed. After playing in the garden, I had to come in through the tradesmen's entrance so as not to disturb Sergei Philipoch unnecessarily. Although bells to summon servants were everywhere, they were not for me and I was taught to observe the same consideration towards all older people. Nor was I allowed to linger in the quarters I thus traversed, but the mysterious running of the house had always fascinated me and now I had a chance to explore.

The laundry-room, where Praskovia was firmly in control, held a special fascination. On the side of her enormous ironing table stood a glass of water which was constantly refilled by a couple of young girls. At regular intervals, Praskovia would take a large gulp from it, blow up her cheeks like some enormous toad she then resembled and, puckering her lips, spit the water in a powerful and finely distributed jet over the linen she was always ironing. Through the steam which rose, I could see Pfouka sitting in a corner, watching the whole proceedings with an expert eye. Pfouka was the oldest inhabitant of the factory almshouse and a great favourite with all. In 1875 when she had first come to work for Grandpa there had been no electricity and it had been Pfouka's job to do the rounds each night, extinguishing all the kerosene lamps. In those days my older cousins had christened her Pfouka, from 'Pf . . . Pf . . .', the sound she made blowing them out! In the lives of the simple, uneducated Russians, ghosts and spirits played an important part, so with the advent of electricity it had been Pfouka's job to persuade her fellow workers that no small devils inhabited the electric bulbs which shone so brightly!

Usually Philipoch, who as butler lorded it over everyone and stealthily went about his job, chased me away. He was a strict disciplinarian, rather like a serjeant-major, and he stood no nonsense from any of the servants, nor from the children. I had not only respect for him but a certain amount of fear. He had been a serf until the age of twelve and his job had been to stand behind his master at meal-times to wave off the flies. Liberated, he came to serve my grandfather, was passed on into our household, and after so many years considered himself rightly a member of it. Closely associated with everything which concerned us, he always spoke of 'our house', 'our life', 'our friends'. When mother was delivered of her first-born, a visitor called to inquire whether the baby was male or female. Philipoch considered the question superfluous and replied with great pride: 'Of course it's a boy. The *barine* and I knew what we were doing!' Now even Philipoch seemed more subdued as he brought from the outside world tales of demonstrations, unrest, police brutalities. . . .

A few months earlier, a member of the French Military Mission had moved into a chalet in our garden. We children soon discovered he had some sort of peculiar installation which greatly intrigued us, as we could sometimes hear the new invention (a wireless) bleeping. From my bedroom windows I saw men in French uniforms come and go; some must have stayed late into the night, discussing problems with my father and uncle and smoking endless cigars, the smell of which gave them away to me next morning when I came down for breakfast.

That year there were the usual big Christmas trees and children's parties. In the hospital, all the wounded were remembered and Tousia and I helped in the wrapping and distribution of presents. There, about that time, Hanochka met an engineer from Toula, her home town. He had been severely wounded and she nursed him with particular devotion. Mama was always teasing her about her 'special invalid'. Before he was sent back to the front, they quietly married. Then she resumed her duties with us and to me, it seemed, nothing had changed. Nine months later she stayed in her room and I was not allowed to see her. Miss Baines, our English governess, took charge of me. I knew better than to ask and anyway direct questions were often met with silence, but when Hanochka finally emerged she was nursing a baby and she said it was her son. Both Tousia and I had seen the doctor arriving with a black bag so it was obvious he had brought the baby to her.

A few days later the child was christened Leo, in honour of Tolstoy, whose Moscow house faced ours. Hanochka used to tell me how in the past he often came to visit and bring us honey from Yasnaya Poliana. My cousin Jane remembered Uncle Paul taking her out of the nursery to 'meet the greatest Russian you will ever see'. To her astonishment, in the drawing-room there was only a *moujik* of large proportions, dressed like countless peasants she had seen! She was about to ask her father for an explanation when the strange man addressed her in the most perfect French and then continued his conversation with her father in the same language.

In the spring of 1917 the Tzar abdicated. There were a lot of guests at our house, drinking champagne, rejoicing and welcoming a change of government, and talking of shocking scandals at Court and disquieting reports from the front. For a few days in Moscow there had been fighting in the streets and I found a piece of shrapnel in the garden. Some of my brothers' companions from the Imperial Lycée had taken part in counter-demonstrations and been shot at, and one of them had been killed. My brothers, eighteen and seventeen, were eager to go into the streets and fight. The French Consul arrived. 'You must have nothing to do with this civil war,' I heard him admonish them. 'If you want to fight, you will do so presently in the French Army against the Germans.'

Hurried arrangements were made and both left for France where they were soon to be called up. Other cousins at school there did not return that year for the usual holidays.

The summer found us again in Himki—for the last time. Conditions were deteriorating fast. I learned words I had not heard before—terror, arrests, search-parties, executions, even torture. In July Papa announced that nationalisation of all industries had been proclaimed by the new régime, another word which had to be explained.

'It will not affect us,' he reassured Mama. 'We are French and this law applies only to the Russians.'

We certainly continued to enjoy our privileged position. Everything of ours was still respected; contented and happy peasants, of whom there were many, bowed, blessed and called Papa *barine* as he went by. Across the span of years how well I recall that last carefree summer with its harvest of yellow corn and the gay sounds of laughing boys and girls as they gathered in the hay during the long, lazy stretching days. With my eyes and nose full of pastoral scenes and country smells the last days of childhood were ebbing away. The weather was particularly warm. With Hanochka busy with her baby son, I was more and more in the care of Miss Baines. Like most English people she was good at sports, loved animals and enjoyed outdoor life, so we played tennis, rode and went for long exploratory walks. Once, surprised by a sudden storm, we sheltered in a hut and then walked back along puddle-ridden paths while crystal drops fell on our heads from the sodden leaves of the tree-lined alleys. Wagtails hopped merrily about, greedily snatching up worms and insects which had come up after the rain.

Miss Baines and I marched in step as she taught me patriotic songs. 'Keep the home fires burning,' she sang. How fortunate it was that we could not imagine the homeless and frightening future ahead! Doubtless thinking of my two brothers and her own, fighting somewhere in France, the last refrain 'Till the boys come home!' always echoed sadly. Yet, far from everything, we did not know that even then, as numerous as the ripe apples falling from the fruit-laden trees, living men were going to their deaths and hopes and ideals were being swept away.

A few days later Mama received a telegram. She read it out to Hanochka in my presence.

'Please tell Miss Baines gently that her brother has been killed in action.'

Mama, upset, discussed with Hanochka how it had best be done.

That evening Miss Baines did not come down to dinner but next morning she played tennis with me as usual.

'Hanochka, why doesn't Miss Baines cry? Didn't she love her brother?' I asked.

'Grown-ups rarely cry when it is a very big sorrow,' she explained.

Most of the guests that summer stayed but a short while. Uncle Kostia talked of terror and famine becoming a reality and of Russian troops at the front now deserting *en masse*. Suddenly soldiers, more bandits than well-disciplined men, made their appearance in the country, until now fairly quiet. They came with requisition slips and led away to slaughter all our cattle and bloodstock. My pony, fat and sleek, did not escape. They left us one cow, a very special concession which would be a godsend with food in short supply. We returned to Moscow on 1 August, a month earlier than usual, and this time there were few peasants to bid us goodbye.

In Moscow, in my brother's bedroom, I found a new addition, a tiny, blue-looking baby who cried incessantly. I was not allowed to touch it, nor did I want to. He was the youngest of Uncle Kostia's children, and for some reason my aunt was unable to look after him.

'This is your cousin Anatole and he is very ill,' Mama said.

For several weeks this unattractive, squeaky little bundle stayed with us. He lay in his cradle, fighting for his life; he was prone to frequent convulsions and it was touch and go for a long time. But Mama's sleepless nights were rewarded and the baby pulled through. Mama had by now become so attached to him that she begged her brother and sister-in-law to let her take the baby to France if the time ever came for us to leave, to which they agreed. Meanwhile he rejoined his parents in the country.

None of us were ever to see Anatole again. Fifty years later when I went back I managed to trace him. He had married the daughter of a prominent communist and his brothers failed to persuade him either to meet me or to talk to me on the telephone. Yet once he had almost become my brother.

Playing in the garden one day I went to the lodge where I kept my sleighs, skates and other paraphernalia. The lodge adjoined the factory wall and the hot pipes running through it kept it warm. On entering it, I saw a young boy sitting there, reading.

'Who are you?' I asked, surprised.

'My name is Genia and I have your father's permission to study here,' he answered, somewhat defiantly, I thought. I also noticed he said 'your father' and not 'the *barine*' as was usual with other factory folk. 'My father is Kousmich, the plumber,' he added, as if to reassure me.

Because my contacts with other children were so carefully scrutinised I thought it extraordinary he should have been allowed here. The Russia in which we lived was one hundred years behind the West and I was sheltered to a degree which, thinking back, appears incredible. I knew nothing of the facts of life or any of life's ugly facets, and in that I was by no means an exception among other children I mixed with. Genia was sixteen, exceptionally quiet and serious and always had his nose in a book. Unknown to everybody he and I became firm friends and I took my young sorrows to him. He soon confessed he was a budding revolutionary (he had to explain what it meant) and he opened up for me a whole new world of poverty and oppression of which I had known nothing.

'Dangerous forces are at work,' he would say as he quoted and tried to explain passages from books he read in secret. Most of these I failed to understand, but I was immensely flattered to have been chosen as his confidante! He swore me to secrecy, which was even more exciting, and when he expended his revolutionary fervour in inflammatory talk I listened fascinated by his stories of an unknown universe—red flags, communists, workers' strikes and all the mixture of violence and fraternity he preached. . . . The ominous was not perceptible to my childish eyes. I was simply watching a kaleidoscope of thrilling and exciting patterns.

Genia's father Kousmich, the plumber, did not approve of his son's new-fangled ideas. Genia complained that he had confiscated some of his books and was always thrashing him for reading them, which I thought very strange because, like most of his ilk, the old man was illiterate. 'But if he cannot read or write,'

I would protest, feeling very sorry for Genia, 'how does he know what is in them?'

To this I received no answer.

'Last night he made me kneel the whole evening in front of the ikon of Our Saviour, to expiate my sins,' Genia complained. 'It was very painful because he had scattered peas on the floor where I had to kneel. You see,' he added, 'I have to suffer for the revolution.'

Genia was very brave and I admired him wholeheartedly. 'Has it occurred to you that the poor are going hungry in spite of ration cards?' he indignantly asked me. I immediately offered to steal food from Philipoch's pantry which he scornfully refused! Shortly after, one morning, I heard gunfire in the distance and did not go to school. Papa gave orders for all factory entrances to be secured.

'We don't want any trouble inside our domain,' I heard him say.

What trouble? I could not imagine. For a girl of eleven it was all very difficult to understand and very bewildering.

In the garden Genia greeted me triumphantly.

'We've done it, we've done it,' he cried excitedly. 'We've formed the Tcheka.'

'What's that?' I asked.

'The Extraordinary Commission for the suppression of the Counter-Revolution,' he replied and started whistling *The Internationale*.

Decidedly, he was not his usual quiet self.

'What Counter-Revolution?'

'Oh, it's no use. You don't understand,' he replied impatiently. 'I can't be bothered to explain everything to you.'

'Don't be nasty, Genia,' I begged.

'I'm not, but you irritate me, always asking questions.' He walked away, he who had always been so patient. I felt let down and more mystified than ever.

Back in the house I found Mama and Hanochka discussing the same events. Something frightening but very exciting was happening. The Tcheka, they said, was an instrument of terror directed against all Russians of education, wealth and social standing. Both were so absorbed in their conversation that they paid no attention to me. I took the opportunity of escaping to the kitchens where Kirianovna always made me welcome because I was her favourite.

'What is it, Kirianovna? What are they all talking about?'

'My poor little *golubka* (little pigeon), don't you worry your pretty little head about it. Nothing can happen to us. Lenin is the anti-Christ and he is preaching the gospel of hate, inciting the poor against the rich! He'll rot in Hell, you'll see. He cannot transform God's Kingdom into a kingdom of evil,' she declared soothingly, restoring at once my sense of peace and security and making her usual sign of the cross over me.

At lunch Papa too was reassuring. Never allowed to talk at table, for once I was not lost in dreams but listened carefully to his conversation with Mama.

'Don't worry, Liouba, we are quite safe and we *are* French. Even the French Government urges me to stay on in order to protect French interests. The new régime is bound to exempt all foreigners from persecution, it's only common sense.'

'But I am worried about Kostia and his family,' Mama replied.

'He'll be all right! At a time like this they'll need legal men to restore order. Besides, if there is really any danger, they can come here. But it won't be necessary, it's only a few hotheads stirring up trouble.'

Just then Philipoch announced Uncle Kostia.

'The situation is deteriorating,' he announced. 'I've sent Miloucha and the children out of Moscow for the time being.'

'What about you? Shouldn't you come here?' Mama sounded worried.

'So far, I'm all right, but the Tcheka has lost no time. Some prominent people have already been arrested.' He cited names.

'What are they being charged with?' Papa wanted to know, a which Uncle Kostia just shrugged his shoulders.

'It's difficult to say, there's chaos everywhere. I was at the Popoffs' last night when a search-party broke in and just requisitioned what appealed to them!'

'How dreadful,' Mama chipped in. 'Could you not protest?'

'You don't realise, Liouba, what conditions are like. I have been told that in Tcheremouchki village some peasants did stand up against the forced requisition of their cattle and were simply shot down wholesale. All the basis of ordinary life is crumbling. There is mass hysteria and shootings in the street are quite common. I strongly advise you not to go out of here for the next few days.'

Philipoch, serving at table, silently nodded. He was in the habit of adding his pinch of salt at family gatherings.

'What are you trying to say, Philipoch?' Mama asked.

'The *barine* is right, *barinia*. I myself saw a riot in the street today. People are very angry, the food shops have been looted so the ration cards are not honoured and they have to go away empty-handed.'

'Thank goodness none of our workers will go short,' Papa commented. 'Our stocks are plentiful and should last at least a month. By that time all this will be forgotten.'

'I would not be so sure,' Uncle Kostia said.

Hanochka, no doubt deciding I had heard enough, made a sign for me to leave the dining-room.

Some days later, Uncle Paul rushed in waving a newspaper.

'There's been an attempt on Lenin's life,' he cried. 'Unfortunately, they missed him but another bolshevik rascal has been shot in Petrograd.' Then he spread the paper in front of Papa.

'Look at this!'

A sensational communiqué by the Tcheka implicated the British Intelligence Service and the French Military Mission in the murder. Thereafter, a procession of French people visited us, people whose importance I would realise only much later. Hanochka said they came to Papa and my uncles because they represented French interests and paid the French Mission's expenses. Some officers of the French Mission were preparing to leave, also Aunt Isabelle with her youngest children and all foreign tutors and governesses, including our Miss Baines. The disintegration of our large family had begun. By the end of the year there remained in Moscow only my parents, Uncle Paul, Hanochka, baby Leo and Tousia and myself. Uncle Paul, deprived of his family, moved in with us.

I had found out that a Workers' Management Committee had been formed in the factory a few weeks earlier at the instigation of the régime.

'They are a friendly lot and devoted to your family,' Philipoch informed me.

Now, for reasons I did not know, that same committee became

powerless to protect Papa and his two brothers and eager to give them a chance to flee, so informed them.

Faithful to his optimistic nature Uncle Paul persuaded his brothers it would only be a temporary measure. 'If they must arrest us, let them,' he said.

Nevertheless, because of his health, Uncle Victor went into hiding to be reunited with us only in France, while Uncle Paul and Papa proceeded to put various affairs in order. This entailed burning compromising documents or those that could be construed as such by some illiterate searcher, and burying treasures in various parts of the grounds and under foundations and walls all over our large domain. This was done at night, when there were no witnesses, a *divertissement* in which Tousia and I played our part. Children could crawl where grown-ups could not and we were both entrusted with endless tin boxes containing God knows what riches and, on our bellies, were told to slide down some underground passage and hide the parcels where no human eye could detect them for years to come and where, eventually, they were to be retrieved! Father followed every such operation by making a detailed plan of the hiding place and then concealing this somewhere else. . . . We did it for quite a while and it became a new and exciting game which compensated me for all my lost playmates. Treasure was also buried by our elders, without our knowledge—proof of which I received fifty years later when a Russian cousin showed me an old cutting from *Pravda* which stated that: 'When mending some underground pipes at the Red Rose factory [they had re-named it almost immediately] forty cases of diamonds, gold and silver had been unearthed—enough to feed the Moscow population for a year!'

Large amounts of money and valuables were also entrusted to faithful workers and servants whose places did not run the risk of being searched. One of these was Kousmich, the father of my revolutionary friend Genia. Genia, meantime, had been conscripted or had voluntarily enlisted into the Red Army and paraded proudly about in uniform. My overtures to him remained unheeded, he wanted nothing more to do with me. I was a member of the hated class. In vain I tried to argue.

'Why can't we be friends, Genia?', I pleaded, deeply hurt. 'We always have been.'

'You are a capitalist, an enemy of the people,' he would

abruptly say and walk away, leaving me baffled. But I was beginning to understand that working-class people and peasants, and only the very poor ones at that, were now in a privileged position and encouraged to order others about—something which I had never been allowed to do. All those who could read and write were liable to be classed as 'bourgeois' and 'bourgeois' became a dirty word and an insult. By a special decree all such people under fifty were commandeered and given the dirtiest menial jobs, while members of the proletariat held the responsible positions. I saw countless *moujiks* gaping at some educated person toiling in the street. I could not understand and never would the sudden gulf between 'us' and 'them'. The ten commandments I had learnt now made no sense. The world I knew had simply been turned upside down, to me it was as elementary as that. I must learn to value things differently, I decided.

In February 1918 Russia signed the peace treaty with Germany. As I went to school, there were soldiers everywhere, returning to their homes, frostbitten, in rags and suffering from exhaustion. The black market for food raged. A decree had been brought in punishing black marketeers with ten years' hard labour, but nobody cared. A few *izvostchik* (cabbies) and their half-starved horses still plied the streets, and a few trams still ran spasmodically and invariably overcrowded, but there was no more private transport, except for the top commissars of the moment. Everything else had been requisitioned. I tramped to school on foot—a novel experience—and I felt very proud because no-one accompanied me!

By another decree our servants had been absorbed into 'national work' and only Philipoch and Kirianovna, exempt by age from compulsory service, stuck to us like glue. The upheaval which had abolished all authority and swept away the old order and traditions had, overnight, also released me from discipline and surveillance. Mother and Hanochka, like everyone else, were doing all sorts of unaccustomed things, so like any street urchin I was free to chase after a peasant's sleigh and, jumping on it from behind, the snow muffling my footsteps, give myself a free ride. I hoped, of course, that such unbecoming conduct would neither be seen by nor reported to Hanochka, but my exuberance at my new freedom knew no bounds.

At school, more and more pupils went missing every day as the

The author, aged 9, a few weeks before the start of the Revolution

Victor Giraud being presented by Czar Nicholas II with a trophy for winning the Prix Imperial of the Automobile Club of Russia, September 1911

Outside the gates of their Moscow house, the author with her father in 1914

fearful epidemic of typhus swept the country. The doors had been opened to a mixed lot of children from working-class backgrounds and boys and girls were lumped together in large classes. A particularly grubby little girl taunted me, calling me a 'dirty capitalist', at which I indignantly protested.

'It's not true, I am not dirty, I wash. But look at yourself, your hands are filthy and your dress is full of spots.'

After this angry exchange, we became friends and I even invited her to visit me, without Hanochka's permission, something I would not have dared before. Philipoch opened the door. He still insisted on protocol, wore his uniform of green cloth and a lot of gold braid and buttons, and with his side whiskers, his gleaming pink bald head and his height he cut an impressive figure. He must have seemed some sort of vision to my little friend who had never encountered so grand a personage!

Totally overcome, she nearly prostrated herself in front of him.

'I did not know your father was a general,' she whispered apologetically and greatly subdued.

'Must you bring such trash to our house? You ought to be ashamed of yourself,' Philipoch grumbled. 'Fancy curtsying to me and taking me for a general. Me, a butler!'

For once his remarks were lost on me. I was being quickly assimilated into a proletarian world and was finding, with a child's unconcern, all kind of advantages and amusements in its relaxed atmosphere. Besides, each day brought new developments and a great deal of bewilderment. By the end of the year, all banks were nationalised, as well as safe deposits where most of Mama's jewelry disappeared overnight. But my parents were not unduly perturbed. An inventory had been made and had been signed by Zinovieff himself, so when times changed for the better, everything would be returned.

The cow which had come back from Himki gave us plenty of milk and Tousia and I watched Kirianovna churn and strain to make butter and cheese.

'Kirianovna, why is there all this just from one cow?' Tousia wanted to know. 'You told me yourself that in the past, in spite of large herds, the bailiff never sent us anything and said the cows went dry in winter?'

But instead of answering Tousia's question, Kirianovna smiled slyly, adding, 'The revolution will teach us all a lot of things.'

Kirianovna had known a great deal of poverty and sorrow. Orphaned as a child of six, she was pushed from place to place, sleeping rough and occasionally being taken in by charitable people. She landed on Grandfather's doorstep and was taken into the kitchens where she remained to run errands for the chef and be a general dogsbody. When Grandpa went to live abroad, she stayed on (no-one ever left) and, having learned the art of cooking from the chef, on his retirement started exercising it with great perfection in our house. She soon became an institution.

On the rare evenings when Hanochka went out Kirianovna, warned by my maid, would steal into my bedroom and, in complete darkness, sit on the floor by my side, ready to hide under the bed if anyone was to come because such visits were strictly forbidden. In a flowery, gentle language she would tell me stories of her vicissitudes, intermingling them with religious stories and fairytales. Tales of joy, grief and superstition succeeded each other, where ghosts and spirits always played an important part—blood curdling stories with no gruesome detail omitted, most of which I knew by heart; but I would make her repeat them again and again and never tired of listening. I was familiar with the evil spirit who lived in the woods and whose loud voice and blazing eyes were enough to fell enormous trees. I knew the Shaggy Water One, with green hair and a blue face, whose home was at the bottom of a lake where he played host to those who drowned. . . .

'Oo, Oo,' she would moan, swaying her body left and right in imitation of a windswept tree. 'Oo, Oo,' she would continue as shudders ran down my spine in excited anticipation. 'A murdered man lies buried here and the tree is screeching and crying, accusing the culprit, you see. It will go on doing so until the terrible crime has been discovered and justice is done.'

'Tell me how you chased the frogs at night,' I would interrupt, longing for her to change the subject which was now giving me goose-flesh. 'Tell me! Tell me!' I would impatiently demand, the story being one of my favourites because I could imagine myself in the rôle.

'Well, it was like this,' she would begin. 'Those frogs were a nuisance to my *barinia*, especially when the moon was up. The silly little creatures mistook the night for day, I should not wonder, and so their concert kept the *barinia* awake all night!

I was only seven at the time, but I was given this important job to do. I had to keep the frogs from croaking.'

'How could you do that?' I would ask, anxious to hear it all over again.

'I would take a leafy lime-tree branch—lime wood bends well, you see,' she would explain, 'and I would chase the little rascals up and down the river bank, flapping the branch about wherever the noise came from. No sooner had I stopped them at one spot, they would re-start at another. Oh, I was kept busy all right,' she would admit with a chuckle. 'Some nights I became so exhausted I fell asleep on the soft grass, wherever I was.'

'What then, what then?' I would insist, anxious for her to finish the story. 'Ah,' she would sigh, 'if I had a particularly successful night keeping the little beasts from croaking and calling to each other, the *barinia* would ask for me next morning and perhaps give me a few kopeks! "Good for you, Natalia," she would say. "The *barine* and I slept well last night. You kept the frogs at bay." '

Kirianovna recalled these moments with obvious satisfaction. The job entrusted to her had been well done. Deeply religious and completely illiterate, she was devoted to us body and soul. The disintegration she was witnessing was incomprehensible to her and she attributed the mass insanity which had taken possession of her land simply and squarely to God's will.

'It does not matter what you do,' she would say, 'everything is predestined.'

I was too young to appreciate whether her spiritual qualities were due to Christian beliefs or to Oriental fatalism. Certainly there was something Asiatic in her acceptance of the situation, yet she was saddened and disgusted, principally for our sake and that of the religious, by the events which were destroying the foundations of home life and moral standards, and she felt strongly that at least the *barine* and his family should be exempt from all torment and privations. As for the Moscow churches, all of which were familiar to her, they were being silenced one by one and no longer tolled continually, and the word 'God' was being erased from everything.

CHAPTER FIVE

Younka was Tousia's French bulldog and a lovable pet. An inveterate fighter, he was feared by all the other dogs. When in a fight his jaw would lock so that he could not let go. The effect of this was often disastrous. His basket stood at the back entrance.

One winter's day, just as dusk was falling, a party of soldiers burst in to the kitchens, guns at the ready. It was yet another search-party. The commotion woke Younka, peacefully asleep in his usual place, and he did his job and barked furiously. Without any compunction whatsoever and before he could be stopped, one of the soldiers shot him in the back. The poor animal, mortally wounded, squealed piteously and ran in circles, to the great amusement of the watching soldiers who jeered and laughed! As Younka's howls brought Hanochka and me running to the kitchens, he fell exhausted, still whining and wriggling. Before I could reach him, another soldier mercifully shot him and then kicked his body unceremoniously into a corner with his boot.

'Younka! Younka!' I cried, as I knelt and put my arms around him. Hanochka tried to drag me away and find the words of comfort, but I would not listen.

'I want Younka!' I howled. 'His eyes are open but he does not move.'

The soldiers just stood there and looked and, all at once, I stopped crying, appalled. I had not yet become accustomed to cruelty and the sight of death. I think at that very moment something crystallised inside me. How could grown-ups, whom I had always considered kind, behave in this way? These men must be my enemies and suddenly I hated them.

Meantime, the search from the servants' quarters up to our rooms proceeded. A few days before there had been an order to surrender all arms under pain of death and, to avoid any possible confrontation, father's guns had immediately been turned in.

However, a pair of antique duelling pistols hanging on the wall of his study had, for some reason, been overlooked. Or maybe he intended to dispose of them later with other valuables and so had flung them into a drawer of his desk and forgotten about it. As he heard the commotion and gathered what it was, he remembered the pistols, but it was too late to do anything about it. Alarmed, he wondered how to divert the searchers' attention from the fateful spot as he watched a soldier systematically empty all the drawers by the simple process of turning them upside down and letting papers fly in all directions. He vaguely saw Philipoch hovering in the background, trying to catch his eye, but he ignored him. However, no pistols fell out, and Papa breathed a sigh of relief!

The commissar in charge, having satisfied himself the house was 'clean', started to withdraw his men when Philipoch, silent until then, announced that Younka had been shot dead.

Upset and angered at this unnecessary cruelty to a family pet, Papa stormed at the commissar.

'Why did you have to kill an innocent animal? What has he done to you?'

The man gave Papa an insolent glance. 'He went for my men. Anyway, he was a bourgeois dog and deserved what he got,' he answered, and walked out followed by his men, amid general consternation and my unrestrained sobbing.

Papa turned to Philipoch, pointing to his desk. 'What happened to my pistols, Philipoch? I clearly remember putting them into a drawer.'

'I saw the bastards coming, *barine*, so I took them out and threw them into the servants' earth closet. They are welcome to look for them in there.' A malicious smile of satisfaction spread over his old, wrinkled face. Then he took me with him to bury Younka in the gardens.

To appease the increasingly vociferous authorities, Uncle Paul put his house at their disposal. He figured it would be requisitioned anyway, so it was just an elegant formula. Half of our home had by now suffered a similar fate and all the reception rooms were meeting-places for various workers' committees. The doors between them and us had been solidly nailed down. The two grand pianos, one in the ballroom, the other in the winter garden, judged by the new masters no longer sufficient, were augmented by five more, looted God knows where. So now, at times, we could hear a note struck with one finger on all seven pianos in turn! Our living quarters considerably reduced, I found it great fun living in close proximity to my parents and their world. Life had become something of a large picnic and without my little maid Groucha to pull on my stockings and put on my shoes, I had to learn to dress by myself. My parents occupied one room, Hanochka and baby Leo a second, Tousia and I a third and Uncle Paul a fourth which served also as the living-room. Philipoch and Kirianovna continued to stay undisturbed in their own quarters and both looked after us with the same unalterable devotion they had practised for more than twenty years. Philipoch insisted on serving the single dish of whatever there was in white gloves, decidedly the worse for wear, while Kirianovna tried to produce some delicacy out of nothing. Uncle Paul, ebullient as ever, rushed about reassuring all those who would listen.

'It's a fact, my dear fellow, it's a fact. All this upheaval cannot last. It will be over in a couple of months, you'll see.'

If present, the two old retainers would gaze at him lovingly and nod their heads in total and silent agreement. They too were sure everything would soon return to its former status.

I now listened eagerly to grown-ups discussing events I had never dreamt of, and fully sharing their life.

'The good old days will return' was a common theme. My parents were not the only ones unable to realise that it was the end of the established order of our Russian life. And it would be my generation's lot to discover that no matter how bad the times, they could always be worse.

My cousin Jane, Uncle Paul's favourite daughter, had always been inclined to go her own way. At heart she was a rebel, and this set her apart from others. She dreamed of a better life for the simple Russian folk to whom she was deeply devoted. Aunt Isabelle was jealous of her husband's preference for this particular child, whom she frankly disliked and he indulged shamelessly. Feeling rejected by her mother, Jane spent most of her time with servants or workers at the factory, who all adored her. This unorthodox behaviour angered Aunt Isabelle still further and, as Jane gradually emerged into attractive womanhood, the antagonism between mother and daughter grew worse. Jane confided this to Mama whom she would always consider her champion. It was to her she had announced in 1915 her intention to volunteer as a nurse in the Russian front lines.

'You don't think I am crazy?' she had asked.

'Of course not. It is a brave and noble thing to do and if I had no family, I would come with you,' Mama had replied.

The decision, however, shocked quite a few people and Aunt Isabelle certainly did not welcome a Florence Nightingale in the family! Her daughter in the trenches with all those *moujiks*—it was inconceivable! Besides, how did she expect to look after the wounded when she had had no training? But, as always, Jane was able to enlist her father's help and he arranged for her to be taught at the hospital of a friend of his. The course lasted six weeks—they were short of nurses at the front. When the order came for her to join her unit, she knew only the few essentials and was, herself, fully aware of her inadequacy. But her devotion to the cause of suffering humanity was such that she felt sure it would teach her all she did not know! She was completely at one with the ordinary people and even talked the imaginative and picturesque dialect of the Russian peasants. She was much more one of them than a member of the French community.

When she left for the front full of youthful enthusiasm, the news she at first sent home reflected her boundless admiration for the courage and stoicism of the Russian soldiers. But as she nursed, comforted and wrote their letters she was shocked to discover their complete illiteracy and ignorance. This only endeared them to her and no doubt stirred her motherly instincts. When, under the exploding shells, she tended the wounded, she was strangely immune to danger. She never spared herself and was happy in her work of mercy. This dedication, which sprung from the unsuspected treasures of her own spiritual self, produced an extraordinary purity and detachment in her which everyone sensed. Attractive, and in some strange way emancipated far beyond her time, she had plenty of opportunities for romance and, no doubt, many suitors, like any girl in a predominantly male society, but she remained firmly aloof from any entanglement. As she was later to tell Mama: 'How could I love anyone in particular when I loved them all so much?'

The war progressed, she was decorated in the field for bravery and wrote to say how touched she had been because, on that occasion, the regimental orchestra had played *The Marseillaise* in her honour. In Moscow, there was talk of the French Government awarding her the *Légion d'Honneur*. Her division had earned itself the title of 'unconquerable' and she was as proud of it as were the fighting men who all treated her as some sort of saint, which amused her because she was a complete agnostic. But when that same beloved division started to retreat, it was a bitter blow. As the turmoil of the cities slowly reached the front, her letters home became less frequent. With the collapse of the Russian resistance and the signing of the peace treaty at Brest Litovsk, there was no more news from her and Uncle Paul worried. Unexpectedly and to his immense relief, she reappeared one day, still wearing her Red Cross uniform and her decorations, but shaken and embittered by the suffering she had witnessed and disgusted by the cruel and often unwarranted behaviour of the men towards their officers. Now she was further upset to find she had no longer a home or a family.

'You had better move in with the girls,' Mama had said, welcoming her with open arms. Tousia and I were delighted to have her share our room. To us she was a heroine and we were fascinated by her stories. 'Kerensky came to the front and preached freedom to the boys, but did he understand what dumb, ignorant children he was dealing with?' she would indignantly ask. 'The poor lads could not even pronounce the word "freedom" correctly,' she complained, flicking her long cigarette holder in all directions as she chain-smoked.

'What an orator he was, Aunt Liouba! But it was only words, words and words. He simply paved the way for the bolshevik propaganda.'

'What did you expect?' came Mama's reply. 'You say yourself all the soldiers were illiterate. Naturally, they are easily twisted and they'll believe anything.'

'But you cannot imagine what those boys had to suffer! I have seen them in the trenches, murdered in their hundreds, holding out against impossible odds, neither armed nor dressed properly! Aunt Liouba, tell me'—she looked pathetically vulnerable and younger than her twenty-one years as she asked the question—'is it possible that all these sacrifices have been in vain?'

'Of course not!' Mama was emphatic. 'Suffering is as necessary to a people as it is to an individual. It helps to understand what life is all about. Out of this a stronger, better Russia will emerge, you'll see.'

'I hope you are right. But I have seen my own men, so unstintingly compassionate and devoted, change completely almost overnight! The appearance of the Red Flag somehow instilled them with a blind, elemental passion which overtook their evangelical kindness. I cannot understand what has happened to their Russian soul, with its special and quite spiritual dimension. You and I know it exists, but where is it now?'

'It still exists and it is this which will pull them through. No other race possesses such Christian humility and inner commitment.'

'How right you are!' Jane exclaimed. 'I never think of the French as having a soul. They only revel in the pleasures of life.'

'Yes,' Mama replied, 'the Russians have always had a deep predilection for suffering.'

'Then how is it that violence has replaced all their wonderful qualities?'

'It won't last,' Mama replied, trying to soothe Jane, who continued to talk. She had to get it all out of her system.

'After Kerensky's visit the morale of our division was reflated. We had all searched for hope amid disaster and he certainly gave it to us. How we waited for the promised offensive to begin! But the orders never came, only subversive agents who preached revolt. At first the men brought their queries to me. They trusted me, you see. "Tell us, Sestriza, whom are we to believe?" What was I to answer? I had tried to do my utmost for them, sharing their fears and their hardships, their rations and their misery. I too wanted a change from the inadequacy of a régime which had sent so many of my friends to their deaths! But how could I be sure this new régime was going to be any better? It was awful to see men now mock their officers and no longer obey them! At first, I even tried to intercede and nearly got lynched. Some of my own men rescued me but it shook me badly. Too many criminals and bandits had joined the troops and I knew I could no longer trust any of them. For the first time I was afraid. There was nothing left but to try and return home,' she concluded sadly.

'You must go to France, this is no longer a place for you, you have done enough as it is,' Mama insisted.

Later, I heard Mama and Hanochka discuss it all.

'She may not have a scratch on her body, but she has been badly scarred just the same. She must feel as if someone had spat into her soul.'

'Yes,' Hanochka had replied, 'it must be awful for her to come back and discover the same hateful rabble in control here where she must have expected to find her usual sanctuary. Her utopian visions of a new Russia have certainly taken a hard knock!'

By this time the exodus of both Russians and foreigners had swollen to enormous proportions but official permits to leave had become more difficult to obtain. Jane insisted on wearing her Red Cross uniform. It gave her considerable immunity in the streets of Moscow and was still respected.

'Papa, you must procure a pass for me to Petrograd. From there on I'll manage somehow,' she told her father.

So eventually a document allowing her to travel there under an assumed name on some imaginary mercy mission was provided by a commissar on Uncle Paul's instigation, probably aided by a thick wad of notes. Bribery was, and would remain, the most powerful weapon in Russia.

The day before her departure we all helped her to pack, or more exactly simply gathered around her for a final reunion! To travel with normal luggage would have attracted attention and therefore she could take only a very few things in her one small suitcase. With a preoccupied air she pondered over her priorities while willing hands padded her clothes with gold and jewels. She would need plenty of both to get her to France!

At the appointed time Uncle Paul accompanied his daughter to the station. The train was already waiting and credentials were being checked before passengers were allowed to board it. At the sight of her uniform and her pass with a special stamp, the young guard said: 'You have the right to claim a seat in a passenger coach.' This was indeed a privilege as most people had to travel in cattle trucks. Clearing a way for her, he led her to the appropriate compartment. Uncle Paul, a familiar figure in Moscow, stood watching his daughter's progress and had no inkling that his presence at the railway station could be misconstrued. Suddenly, one of the guards recognised him and raised the alarm.

'Stop him, stop him, he's escaping!'

Within seconds Jane saw her father surrounded by soldiers

and bundled out of her sight but not before he had time to turn round and shout in French: 'For God's sake, don't let them know who you are!'

Three years were to pass before father and daughter would meet again.

CHAPTER SIX

In October 1918, under cover of darkness, a young officer of the French Military Mission moved all the wireless equipment from the chalet of our garden into the flat of Mr R, a member of the French colony, whose apartment on the Loubianka was next door to the Tcheka. 'They are unlikely to search on their own doorstep,' Uncle Paul told Papa. Because we now lived in such close proximity I knew it had required considerable ingenuity to get the cumbersome installation to a third-floor flat without arousing anyone's suspicion. From there, it seems, transmissions were able to continue for several more weeks and Papa and my uncle discussed all this freely in front of me thinking that I would not understand a lot, and anyway we had all learned to keep our mouths shut.

The positively last train for the evacuation of British and French nationals was due to leave Moscow on 15 December and Mr R, his wife and his daughters were to travel on it. The girls were our friends so naturally we talked of nothing else.

'We'll have to move the wireless equipment again,' Papa had commented. But at the end of November there was a night raid on Mr R's flat, the wireless was discovered and he was taken away for questioning. His wife, in a hysterical condition, came running to our house.

'Mon Dieu,' she sobbed, 'we should have left before! If Eugene misses this last convoy, what will happen to us?'

'Calm yourself, Madame.' Uncle Paul reassured her with every bit as much optimism and confidence as usual. 'I am sure he will not be long detained. Remember, when Jane left I too was arrested, but they released me after twenty-four hours! It will be the same for Eugene, you must not worry.' But she burst into such a paroxysm of tears that I was quite alarmed.

'Suppose they don't let him out in time to catch the train? They may even accuse him of espionage because of your wireless. Monsieur, you must do something. I am not leaving Russia without him!'

'I promise to do what I can. And there is no question of espionage, Madame. We have to communicate with our government. Unfortunately there are so few left whose help I can enlist.'

'Then I shall go myself to the Loubianka,' Madame R threatened. My uncle shook his head. Madame R's Russian always made us laugh, it was rudimentary in the extreme, she mispronounced words and he obviously doubted it could be of any use. But politely he did not tell her so. Discussions as to what to do continued for some time while I sat in a corner pretending to read. Finally they decided that Mary, Mr and Mrs R's eldest daughter, nineteen years old, should pose as her father's wife and, by playing on some commissar's compassion, extricate him on a forty-eight-hour parole from prison under the pretext of saying goodbye to his family. ·

'I assure you her youth and good looks will do the trick and we can then bundle him on to the train,' Uncle Paul said. 'It is quite on the cards that his disappearance will not even be noticed for several days. Only the timing is all-important. She must manage to obtain his release on the 13th or 14th, to give him a fair chance.'

We later listened to Mary being briefed and then she confided to us her excitement and her fears. She felt keenly that the success or failure of the operation was firmly and squarely on her young shoulders. By tramping to various places of detention she soon found out that her father had been transferred to the Andronevsky Monastery which stood at one of the old gateways to Moscow. This was encouraging. It meant that his crime was not viewed too severely, or maybe he had persuaded his gaolers that he had nothing to do with the wireless installation, which the Russians claimed was for espionage purposes. (It probably was.) For several days Mary acted the rôle of the abandoned young wife left alone with her children, but although she evoked the necessary sympathy, she made no progress.

'You should see Comrade Djerjinsky, he's the only one who could help you,' an official suggested.

Djerjinsky was omnipotent, we all knew it. It was he who signed all the death warrants and the thought alone sent shivers down her back. But time was short, so she lined up at Djerjinsky's office to beg for an interview with him. Probably Uncle

Paul was right and her appearance helped, because a few days later she was ushered in to the presence of that frightening genius of evil. She was surprised to find him quite pleasant although he had a cruel, hard face. He listened to her plea for parole almost sympathetically.

'You are very young to have three children,' he remarked.

Scared out of her wits by being in the presence of Djerjinsky, Mary told us she burst into uncontrollable tears.

'Your request seems quite reasonable,' she heard him say. Maybe he could not stand hearing a woman crying. Who knows?

He quickly scribbled something on a piece of paper, signed it and handed it to her. The interview was over and it had all been so easy. Still frightened and hardly believing her luck she rushed home and showed us the pass she had obtained only just in time. It was 13 December and she would have to move fast if she was to bring her father safely home. A false beard had already appeared from somewhere to give him a better chance of not being recognised. Now Mrs R refused point-blank to pack. She was in a state of complete nervous collapse. She would not take more than one small suitcase between the five of them because she was afraid to attract in some way the notice of the soldiery whose insatiable desire to loot might lead to their discovering her husband's identity!

It was dark and very cold by the time Mary boarded a tram to the end of the line. From there, she had to walk some distance to the gates of the monastery. Two sentries were standing guard, she could just see their shadows. Immediately, she was halted. More dead than alive, she replied: 'I have come to fetch my husband on a forty-eight-hour parole by order of Comrade Djerjinsky.' The men were visibly taken aback to see a young woman alone on such a dark night. They inspected her and the permit with great suspicion. Then a slit opened in the heavy gates and she was handed over to a guard. Without a word he escorted her across a yard past other sentries and into a large, grey building. They were inside the monastery itself. Here, in a sort of hall, a man with a red armband sat at a table. He too scrutinised the permit, held it up to the light and even used a magnifying glass. Satisfied it was genuine, he made a sign to the soldier. She was led still further, through a faintly illuminated darkness, until they came to some stone steps at the bottom of which stood two enormous church candelabra with lit candles, which added to the eeriness of the surroundings. She wondered whether the steps led to a monk's cell? This had been a monastery. Or maybe this was some kind of trap? Trembling and chilled to the marrow, she followed the man. He stopped at the top, turned a huge key in the door confronting him and pushed her in. She was in a large room with about thirty men in it. There was a sudden hush as all eyes turned on her. She saw men in military uniforms but with epaulettes torn off, she recognised a priest although his cassock was, for some reason, cut off above the knee. Then she saw her father sitting in a coffin. Was this a dream? She noticed a number of coffins lined up against the walls. In some of them men were asleep, in others they just sat. She was not to know that these coffins had belonged to the monks, whose custom it had been to bury their own dead. Now they were being used as bunks and to give the prisoners warmth and protection from the stone floors.

She flew to her father. He was still wearing the coat with a beautiful fur collar in which he had been taken away. She saw the frightened look of surprise—he evidently thought she too had been arrested. Then she was in his arms, kissing him and whispering. 'Papa, I have come to fetch you on parole. But I am not your daughter, I am supposed to be your wife!'

He replied immediately, in a loud composed voice: 'Little wife, I am so happy to see you. We are very comfortable here and they treat us well,' but his eyes belied the praise, he looked grey and old and she sensed he was afraid.

'You are coming home with me. Look, I have the pass!' and she showed him the magic paper.

Still he did not seem convinced, something was holding him back and she could not understand it.

'We had better stay here,' he pleaded. 'It is so cold outside. Why not stay here at least the night?'

This is incredible, Mary thought. She had laboured so hard, schemed and lied and now this resistance. The priest, standing apart, edged nearer and looked over her father's shoulder.

'It must be all right, Evgeni Stepanovich,' he quietly said. 'After all, it does bear Djerjinsky's signature and they would not dare . . .' he added, ominously. Later, it transpired that a prisoner had been shot in similar circumstances under the pretext that he was trying to escape.

65

'Come, come,' Mary pleaded, pulling her father towards the door where the guard stood waiting. He stepped aside to let them pass and she retraced her steps, holding tightly to her father's hand. In the hall, a column of prisoners under heavy armed guard was being assembled for night work, which consisted of picking up people and animals who had died of starvation in the streets. The humans were taken to a common grave, the animals, such as dead horses, served to augment the rations of the starving people.

Outside the monastery they hailed a solitary cabby returning in the direction of the town, and thus they reached the apartment. Mrs R threw herself into her husband's arms, crying: 'Oh, Eugene, I never thought I would see you again.'

A few weeks after Mr R's successful departure, on a cold winter's night in 1919, we were woken at about 2am by the opening of the gates, the sound of marching feet and the sound of a lorry being driven in to the courtyard. We gathered in my parents' room, anxiously awaiting developments. There was loud banging on the front door and a prolonged ringing of the bell as if someone was trying to pull it off. A few seconds later I heard Philipoch hurrying to the door. Soldiers, who must have brushed past him, burst in, bayonets at the ready and guns bristling, and invaded our privacy. Immediately the search began. Mattresses and pillows were ripped apart, furniture overturned and cupboards emptied, looted and broken in the process. Some of the soldiers appeared quite drunk and I saw one stuff his pockets with whatever took his fancy. Huddled close to Hanochka and my parents, I was petrified by such inexplicable and frightening behaviour. After about twenty minutes, having turned our rooms upside down, Papa and Uncle Paul were ordered to get dressed and, like a couple of criminals, were driven away in the waiting truck. They had committed the double sin of being capitalists and foreigners. We were left behind, trying to tidy up and sort out the horrible mess.

Next morning the familiar Factory Committee, judged no doubt too lenient, was replaced by a hard-faced commissar and his no-less-frightening minions. Now the harassment began in earnest. I was no longer allowed to play in the garden but was confined to our rooms and school. Mama's and Hanochka's movements were constantly watched and we seemed to be under

Claude Giraud, founder of the Giraud Factory, with his two sons and the rest of the factory management. Victor is on his father's right and Andrew, the author's father, on his left

The Giraud Factory compound included the family's house and gardens with living accommodation for the entire workforce of 4000 which had increased to 10,000 by 1914

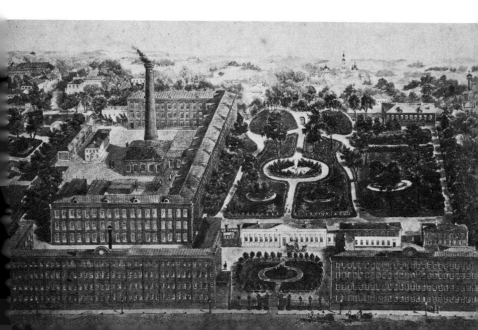

(Above) The female workers' dormitory and *(below)* the dining room in which the employees were fed

some sort of house arrest. This lasted only a short time and one morning Papa and Uncle Paul reappeared unexpectedly at the breakfast table! The new management put in by the soviets to run the factory had proved incompetent, so now we witnessed the strange sight of Papa and Uncle Paul arriving to their respective offices from prison every morning, very much the bosses during the day, to be taken back there at night like criminals. Everything was possible in those days and this strange procedure was quite common as people with technical qualifications were often let out just to do some essential job. Nevertheless, this new arrangement raised hopes that perhaps things were improving. Then they both disappeared again and this time no-one knew where they had been taken.

Days of torment passed and Mama's inquiries as to their whereabouts yielded nothing. Most of her Russian friends had either been arrested or were in hiding. Uncle Kostia had been sent by his new masters out of Moscow so even his consoling presence was denied her. Aided by faithful Hanochka she continued her fruitless search and both queued for hours at various prison gates in the hope of gleaning some information—all to no avail.

Returning home one day from some errand, I found several women I had never seen before raiding my mother's cupboard and helping themselves to her clothes. They had broken into our sanctuary from the requisitioned part of the house. As one of them turned round, I recognised Emilia, Mama's personal maid, conscripted by the régime into another job some time before. Flabbergasted, I watched while she tore Mama's best furs out of her companions' hands, insulting them meantime for all she was worth.

'These are for me, you bitches,' she screamed. 'I spotted these long before you set your filthy eyes on them. I haven't slaved in this house for nothing, these are mine, I tell you,' and grabbing her loot she swept past me, the others following in her wake. Dumbfounded, I just stood and stared. How could Emilia, whom Mama had always trusted, act that way? Mama had always been kind to her. What would she say when I told her of such disgusting behaviour?

Mama disbelieved my story.

'It could not have been Emilia,' she kept repeating, and

Hanochka joined in. Both tried to persuade me I had been mistaken, but I stuck to my guns.

'It was Emilia, I know,' I stubbornly insisted. 'Perhaps she was cold and needed a coat,' I added on the spur of the moment, trying to find an excuse for her.

We were still arguing and Mama was bemoaning the girl's ingratitude when the door was flung open and Emilia herself burst in, still clasping the furs to her bosom. She threw herself at Mama's feet. '*Barinia*, dear *barinia*, you always told me to take good care of these furs as they were your best. Tell me I have saved the right ones from those fiends.'

It then transpired that she had overheard the women's plot to invade our rooms and had followed them in, pretending to be a looter and a privileged one at that!

'I have never laid my eyes on any of these women before, *barinia*,' she indignantly assured Mama. 'They have come from outside. There is no-one here who would have behaved like that.'

One evening while I was preparing my lessons for the morrow the nasty-faced commissar barged in without preamble and informed Mama that we were to vacate our rooms.

'We are requisitioning the whole house,' he announced.

'But where are we to go?'

'We are providing lodgings for you in Novoya Dimitrovka. You have until 3pm tomorrow and you are to take only the strict minimum.'

'What do you mean by that?' Mama asked. She realised the position quite clearly and was torn between indignation and consternation but she was not letting the man see her discomfiture, so remained composed and rather aloof. He might have been talking about the weather and not turning a defenceless woman and her children out of their home.

'I mean four beds, four chairs, a table and whatever else may be required for your comfort.' There was mockery in his voice as he spoke the last words. But four beds meant that Hanochka could come with us and secretly Mama rejoiced.

'A horse and cart will be put at your disposal by the committee to transport such belongings as you will be allowed to take,' he added. Then, probably annoyed to see her seemingly unperturbed, he abruptly turned on his heels and left.

For some reason in all cataclysms one's mind turns to rela-

tively unimportant matters. Maybe it is a protective mechanism.
Now, no doubt deeply upset by the commissar's orders, Mama
and Hanochka seemed to have one idea only, to save Grandpa's
priceless library of antiquarian books.

'Come on children,' Hanochka said, 'help carry these upstairs
into the small room by the attic where they can be under lock
and key.'

Of course I wanted to know why.

'They will be safe there until we come back.'

By some extraordinary oversight the little room harbouring the
treasures my godfather had showered upon me had not yet
attracted any attention.

'Why are we going then, if we are to come back?' I continued
my questions with the deadly logic of a child.

I was told to shut up and help. Philipoch and Kirianovna also
lent a hand as Tousia and I rushed up and down the stairs carrying enormous leather-bound volumes. With infinite care Mama
and Hanochka arranged these on shelves while we carried on our
shuttle service. When the bustling and excitement had completely
exhausted me, I was sent to bed while the sorting of what we were
to take went on into the night. But when the commissar next
morning saw what had been stacked, he shouted: 'Nothing is to
go out of these rooms. The furniture is to be taken only out of the
servants' quarters.'

Busy sorting out a few favourite toys, I spotted on the mantel-
piece a china figure of a bulldog which looked like Younka. I had
not been allowed to touch it in the past but now I sensed my
opportunity.

'Can I have it, Hanochka?' I begged.

No doubt preoccupied by more important issues and to my
immense joy she silently nodded. I picked up the precious orna-
ment and, leaving my box of toys for her to deal with, hurried
towards the exit where, at the top of the stone steps, the commissar was supervising the loading. Seeing me he barred the way.

'What have you got there?' he asked.

But I was not prepared to surrender. The bulldog was mine,
Hanochka had allowed me to take it. Mama, I knew, hated this
nasty man so why should I give up something which belonged to
her?

'It's mine,' I said, backing away from him. I felt cornered and my heart was thumping. Suddenly I remembered how easily in the past I had smashed the French dolls Papa bought me and so, as he stretched out his hand, my untamed instinct got the better of me and I dropped the china figure where I stood and watched it shatter into a thousand pieces.

'It's all your fault,' I cried, scared to death of what he might do to me. But at that very moment his attention was distracted by workers from the factory who, sensing something was wrong and heedless of his invectives, were pushing their way into the house with offers of help. They were rallying to us in our hour of need. Soon they were helping to load the waiting cart with a few of our miserable possessions while sullen guards stood and watched. Two large portraits of my grandparents which used to hang in the hall had been fixed to the back of the cart, by whom and why we never did discover. Now I witnessed an unbelievable sight. One by one from the assembled crowd men and women came to the back of the cart and, dropping on their knees, crossed themselves and kissed the portraits as if they were some miraculous ikons.

'They remember all your grandparents did for them,' Hanochka softly whispered, visibly touched.

'But why do we have to leave then?' I asked.

'It is only temporary,' she replied, which made it all the more incomprehensible.

The commissar, livid at this spontaneous demonstration, gave the order for the horse and cart to be on the move. Reminiscent of a funeral procession, we trudged behind it. Some of the women ran after us, kissing the hems of our coats. Others were crying unashamedly. I remember one ot the cart's wheels must have needed greasing because it squeaked and made a funny accompaniment to their sobs.

And so we walked out of our impregnable domain carrying an odd assortment of possessions. 'Don't leave any of your pets around, we don't want useless vermin,' the commissar had said. So Tousia was clasping her Angora cat while I carried my large teddy bear and a small jar into which I had put a goldfish. Mama, whom I had never before seen carrying anything, was laden like a camel but, nevertheless, held her head high, and Hanochka with baby Leo made up the rear. From our luxurious home we came out little better than beggars and were forced to exchange it for a dark, damp hovel consisting of two rooms, a kitchen and a WC. This new home was unimaginably squalid and not even clean. Our arrival disturbed a horde of cockroaches which scattered in all directions with the rapidity of lightning.

'It could have been worse,' was Mama's only comment. 'At least it is not a communal apartment.' How I admired her at that moment!

Shortly after, when Uncle Kostia returned to Moscow, he found his house too had been requisitioned, but he was given a room in it. He it was who found out that Papa and Uncle Paul were in Boutirki Prison. But very soon he also was arrested. Mama immediately wrote to Aunt Miloucha, urging her to return so as not to lose Uncle Kostia's precious room, but events now moved so fast that the two sisters-in-law were never to meet again.

By now we were becoming accustomed to all sorts of deprivations and Hanochka used all her ingenuity in inventing ways to overcome them. For instance when my only pair of *valenkis* (felt boots) wore out, she made me some out of an old piece of carpet. When my mittens were stolen at school, she took some sacking, made two small bags with thumbs and then showed me how to stuff these concoctions with newspaper and put my hands in to keep them warm. I strutted off delighted, too young for any regrets. Even Papa's arrest had no immediate impact on me. He was in prison because he was a capitalist and a Frenchman and I was proud to think he was as important as that! But hunger and awful chilblains were more difficult to ignore. There was nothing anybody could do about it and I really suffered.

In our miserable home we were also hopelessly overcrowded. Hanochka was having more and more difficulty in feeding baby Leo. Our cow had been taken from us and baby-food had completely disappeared, as had practically everything else. It was a red-letter day when she managed to barter a dress for oatmeal, only to find it badly infested by fat little maggots. After some thought, she cooked it, maggots and all, to add, as she explained, proteins to his already depleted diet. She worried constantly about his health and the future decidedly looked grim. Every day it became more evident that it would be more prudent for her, a Russian, to dissociate herself from us and leave Moscow for a while. But she was very reluctant to abandon Mama at such a time and was torn between her loyalty to her and her husband who, back from the war in Toula, not unnaturally urged her to join him, assuring her that famine and life's conditions were not as acute there.

After a lot of soul-searching and heartbreaking discussions it was decided she must go. In vain Hanochka tried to persuade me our separation would not be for long. I felt she was forsaking me. I loved her more than anyone else and, at that time, certainly more than my parents whom I was only beginning to know. She had brought me up, taught me all I knew and her authority was the only one I recognised. Yet I understood that for her too, it was not easy. She had been with us for close on twenty years—to me, this was forever—but if she were to remain, her very life would be in danger. All this she patiently explained, but the pain I experienced seemed unbearable, probably because it was the first of many heartbreaks. Nothing ever could repay Hanochka's constant devotion but Papa and Uncle Paul were determined it should not go unrewarded. 'If you wish to do something,' she had quietly said, 'then please obtain for me a railway ticket to Toula.'

It is impossible to imagine what such a request meant at that time! Russians were fleeing the country wholesale, they were willing to endure privation and even death rather than live under Soviet rule. The régime knew it well, and to purchase a ticket to anywhere was by now almost impossible. All transport had broken down and the few trains that did run were full to over-flowing. But money and influence could still achieve miracles and Uncle Paul still had plenty of both. To him, all obstacles seemed insignificant. A few days before his arrest he left instructions for this gift to be handed to her when the time came. How could he imagine this would be the last service he would be able to render this selfless woman whom not one of us would ever see again.

I still recall the day when, blinded by tears, I pulled my sleigh with her suitcase on it to the station along the snow-covered Moscow streets while Tousia helped to carry baby Leo in whose clothes we had sewn our last available stock of camphor to protect him against the lice. Mama stayed behind—she could not face the parting. Nor do I rightly remember it. The only image which remains is of a train black with people hanging from it in all directions, puffing its way out of snowbound, hungry Moscow and carrying away with it the remnants of my happy childhood.

Hanochka's departure left a void which, I thought, nothing could ever fill. Shielded and protected by her, I had been a little girl that morning. But with the first ache of loneliness which invaded me, I suddenly realised I was no longer a child.

CHAPTER SEVEN

Now we were three. Mama was wonderfully courageous and she never complained. There was plenty Tousia and I could do to help. Red terror had become a reality unleashed with a ferocity that only Slavs could produce. Impoverished and hungry, we lived in constant fear for ourselves, for those friends who were still at liberty and principally of course for Papa, Uncle Kostia and Uncle Paul. If they were to survive the disease and the hunger in prison, food parcels were essential. This meant endless waiting in queues, in which all three took part in turns, and a constant search to buy something on the rampant black market. Between attending school, hunting for provisions and lining up at the prison gates our days were fully occupied. I cannot explain logically anything I did at that time. At first unhappy at having lost Hanochka I soon became intoxicated with my new-found freedom and began to learn a lot of things which, thinking back, I would have gladly left unlearned!

To school and back Tousia and I had to walk five miles. On the Pritchistensky Boulevard one day we sat down on a bench to rest. A man beside us was reading a paper. We were both so naïve that nothing ever presented any danger. We went on chatting merrily, discussing school affairs, when suddenly the man folded his paper and leered at us. In his lap we saw something resembling a large, red sausage. He was smiling broadly and something in his smile scared the life out of us. Clasping hands, we jumped up like a couple of scalded kittens and ran in the direction of the Church of Our Saviour, not stopping until we got there. Panting, we sat on a nearby wall.

'What was it?' I asked.

'I don't know,' Tousia replied. 'Some sort of sausage, but why did he show it to us?'

'It looked as if it was stuck to him,' I commented.

Tousia nodded. 'Did you notice the way he looked at us? It was horrible. We'd better not tell anybody about it, we shall keep it a secret from grown-ups. Mama always says we must not loiter,' she added.

Both of us would remember the incident years later, but at the time our education had been such that, although sixteen and twelve, we were completely ignorant.

When my turn came to take a food parcel to the prison I rushed there at full speed. How long it took to deliver depended on the length of the queue. But on the way back I could linger as Mama would attribute any delay simply to the fact that I might have had a long wait. Stopping everywhere, peeping into courtyards, looking through windows of houses, investigating thoroughly a world which was abruptly changing and which I had now discovered, I was getting a real taste of what life was all about—at least I thought so. The metamorphosis from a nicely brought-up little girl into a young hooligan was very rapid. The new ways of a gipsy existence were fascinating and I was quickly becoming a rootless child of the revolution. A desire lurked deep inside me to perform some anti-social act which Hanochka would have checked by education, sanity and moral sense. But there was no Hanochka and Mama had so many worries it was increasingly difficult for her to keep a constant eye on me.

Returning from running an errand, I came across a little hillock on the outskirts of the town where I could rest hidden from view by bushes. I could look out over a sort of field or waste ground bordered by trees and a ditch. At that time transport was free but the existing trams were so full that I could never succeed in boarding one, no matter how hard I pushed! So I walked long distances—often on an empty stomach. Now I sat down to rest, thinking of nothing in particular, when I saw in the distance some soldiers with five or six people. I looked on, and what happened made no special impression on me. I have often wondered about it since and can only deduce I could not have grasped its significance. The soldiers, I thought, were attending some kind of manœuvre and, for some strange reason, lined up the people they had brought. There was a short burst of fire, the people disappeared and only the soldiers remained. Was it some conjuring trick? Spellbound, I watched the military depart. I returned home with an untroubled mind and even forgot to mention what I had seen, but next time I went to the prison, some mysterious force dragged me to the same spot where I again sat down and waited. An unwholesome curiosity had taken possession of me and I wanted to find out what those soldiers really did. Ten minutes went by. The waste ground lay at my feet about two hundred yards away. It was surrounded by barbed wire and I wondered whether the field was reserved for military exercises? Nothing more sinister occurred to me. I was about to give up and go home when there were the soldiers again and with three women and four men. I crouched behind the bush and this time watched carefully what was going to happen. I heard one of the women cry out and saw her break away, but a soldier pulled her back towards the others reassembled under guard near the ditch. I became really interested. Extraordinary as it may seem, I did not realise people were being shot. I watched the spectacle like some fantastic Grand Guignol presentation, noticing only that the men fell straight and rigid and the women collapsed like deflated balloons. I kept the incident to myself but a few days later I was back, waiting for the show to begin, and then appraised the behaviour of the participants with a critical eye. If one resisted, I thought how stupid since the result was a foregone conclusion. To this day I fail to understand how I could have been so callous. I had, of course, witnessed terrible sights and perhaps had become accustomed to the sight of death.

Once, coming home later than usual, Mama asked me where I had been. With no sense of shame, I recounted in detail the scene I had witnessed.

'How long have you watched this?' Mama asked, her voice strangely dead-pan.

'About half-a-dozen times. I can always tell by the way they fall whether it is a man or a woman,' I added proudly.

An unbelieving look of horror came over Mama's face. 'Do you mean to say you have been coolly watching people being shot and to you it has been some sort of entertainment? What sort of little monster are you? You cried disconsolately when Younka was shot and now human lives mean nothing? Do you realise that it might have been members of your own family?'

She fairly blazed at me. Her lovely grey-green eyes grew wider and flashed with anger as she stood accusing me. I had never seen her in such a state. I listened to her diatribe and did not answer. It had not been like that at all. I had simply wanted, like some curious little animal, to discover something I was not meant to see. I did not think it was cruel and horrible and felt myself wrongly accused. But at last her words came home to me. 'Forgive me, forgive me, I did not know,' I sobbed.

There remained a small church not far from where we lived which still held services. Worried by remorse and anxious to put this experience out of my mind, I asked Kirianovna (who still visited us) to take me there. At the corner of a street we came upon what was now a familiar and degrading sight. Two very young soldiers were mocking an elderly priest. They had knocked off his head-gear and were playing football with it. When the old man tried to retrieve it, they mercilessly pulled his beard.

Kirianovna, fearless in her indignation, advanced towards them, shaking her fist. 'You Godless hooligans, you scum! Your mothers should be ashamed to have brought you rascals into this world! God will punish you! Be off, you louts!' she screamed.

Her outburst stopped the horseplay and one of the youths turned round. 'Genia!' I cried, and without a moment's hesitation, forgetting he was one of the culprits, I rushed towards him. I had not seen him since we had been turned out of our home, and I was overjoyed. But the young soldier who confronted me gave me an icy stare, said something to his companion and both walked away adjusting their caps leaving me standing in complete dismay. The priest collected himself, blessed us and went on his way. Kirianovna grabbed my hand tightly and dragged me off reciting prayers aloud.

I too prayed all the way to the church with unaccustomed fervour. I was scared. The confusion was growing daily. Night arrests were a regular feature—dark deeds, I was told, are better done at night. Terrible mistakes occurred constantly. At school that morning, one of my newly acquired friends sat in a corner, a picture of desolation, crying disconsolately. She came from an obscure family and bore a very ordinary Russian name, so ordinary that it should have been a protection. They were neither rich nor famous, neither aristocrats nor intellectuals. Yet the militia came in the night, she told me, and took away her father. Her mother tried to tell the soldiers it must be a case of mistaken identity. 'Don't worry, Ma, they'll sort it all out at the Loubianka,' said the soldiers. But she did worry. At the Loubianka next morning they told her that her husband had been shot.

'There's been a mix-up of Christian names. We wanted Nikolai. You say your husband's name was Vladimir? Bad luck,
citizen.'

What did it matter that her mother was left a widow with seven
children to bring up? What is one life when you are trying to
remake a country?

On a sunny October day in 1919, as I was preparing to go to
school, Mama, whose existing clothes had become decidedly
shabby, went out to visit her dressmaker. In the hectic events of
the last year she had neglected to pick up a skirt which would be
more than welcome now.

I came home in the late afternoon to find Tousia alone and
very upset. 'Mama has been arrested,' she said.

'Where? How?' I suddenly felt weak at the knees.

'I don't know. Tania was walking down the Arbat to her chem-
istry lesson when she saw Mama going by in a cab with a strange
man. She was about to wave when Mama raised herself in her
seat and cried out: "Tell my daughters that——" Tania did not
hear any more. The man clapped his hand over Mama's mouth
and pushed her back into her seat.'

We looked at each other. 'What are we going to do?' I
asked.

'I don't know. Perhaps once her identity has been established
they will let her go.'

All night we waited but she did not return. As soon as it was
daylight we hurried to the nearest police station. They had no
information and suggested we go to the Loubianka. There, they
either knew nothing or did not want to tell us and sent us to
Boutirki Prison. But no-one knew anything anywhere. We spent
another night completely bewildered and feeling abandoned and
lost. We did not know what to do and all sense of security
vanished. Mama had just disappeared.

The following morning there was a knock on the door and in
came a man wearing the dreaded red armband and announced
that he was the district commissar. He had three soldiers with
him and he ordered them to guard us day and night. We had
heard of this procedure, which had been prevalent for some time.
When someone had been arrested, their home was invaded by
guards who remained for some time to ambush those that came
to visit. Mama must have fallen into a similar trap. People were

becoming wise and only called on each other with great circum-
spection.

The men squatted on the stone floor and at once occupied
themselves by playing cards and smoking, littering the floor all
around. They were rough and dirty but not unkind, and we were
lucky because certainly they did not harm us in any way and did
not attempt to rape us. We were so completely ignorant on all
sexual matters that perhaps our very innocence may have been
our greatest protection. The men showed compassion and even
shared with us their meagre rations, mostly dry fish (*vobla*) which
they carried wrapped in newspaper in their rucksacks, next to
foul tobacco.

It was very cold in the flat. When they saw we had no wood,
one of them went out and came back with lovely logs he had
requisitioned on sight from a passing peasant. The fire he lit
blazed merrily and threw out such heat that my chilblains began
to itch terribly. I had to take off my *valenkis*, exposing such
lacerated feet and burst sores that even these hardened men
commiserated. After that we became friends and they even told
us that Mama had been taken to the Loubianka. Like most simple
folk they had no love for the Soviet régime but they were too
ignorant and backward to know how to resist it effectively.

We were not supposed to leave the flat or to communicate
with the outside world, but the men relented and let me out on
the pretext of buying apples. Briefed by Tousia, I ran to Olga
Vasilievna, Mama's friend and the mother of Tania and Lera
who were both at school with us, warning them not to call.

After five days, bored no doubt by waiting for prey which never
materialised, the soldiers left, but not before they had told us
plenty of horrifying stories of murder, pillage and vengeance
which made me hate the new rulers and greatly impressed
themselves on my mind.

We were now left to our own devices in a country ravaged by
civil war and famine. Few could help—all had their own troubles
and to associate with foreigners was unhealthy. Philipoch and
Kirianovna, weakened by hunger and age, lived at the other side
of the town and could not call very often. We would have to use
our inventive talents if we were to survive. Although frightened,
we were at the same time excited. We were very lucky by the
standards of those days to have the privacy of our miserable home.

Most people like us lived in communal apartments or even in rooms, sharing a kitchen and washing facilities, with all the discomfort that entailed.

It was a very cold winter, all the pipes were frozen and, for water, we had to bring in buckets of snow from outside. We again had no heating, most of the scant furniture had been chopped up for fuel and the thermometer in the place registered one degree above zero. The cold felt all the more intense because we were always hungry. There was no question of undressing in such a temperature. We slept in the same bed, huddled together for warmth and with everything we could find piled on top of us as we discussed which was the deadlier enemy—cold or hunger? Rats made an occasional sortie, looking for food. They were enormous and often I would wake up to see one of these repulsive creatures sitting at the bottom of our bed, staring with incredible boldness. We had constantly to shoo them off, and I was very afraid that they might be after my sores. I had heard of them attacking sick or dying people, and a neighbour's baby left alone in its cradle for five minutes had been badly bitten.

A little girl of six called Bunchy lived with her grandmother two doors away and also fetched snow from the yard. This forged a link and sometimes I would go and help her with her reading. From the grandmother I learned that Bunchy's father had been killed in the war, but I never found out what happened to her mother. The old lady and the little girl were inseparable. They lived in a dark corner of a room in a communal apartment and there, in abject poverty, Bunchy slept in the old woman's bed and in her arms for warmth. One morning, after a particularly frosty night, Bunchy woke up feeling very cold. As was her habit she snuggled up to her grandma but the old lady had died in the night and *rigor mortis* had set in. Bunchy was too young to realise that her grandmother had starved to death, so she shook the old lady and called out to her. Not getting any response she came running to us.

'I can't wake Grandma up, please come and help,' she pleaded.

By the time Tousia and I came on the scene, the other occupants had discovered what had happened. The police were informed, the old lady's body was carted away, but what was to be done with Bunchy no-one knew. Somehow she found herself with us and sleeping in our bed, but after a few days a militiaman came to take her away. Tousia was out, Bunchy cried and clung to me. She did not want to go with a strange man although, I remember, he was kind and tried to explain to us the best way he could that he was taking her to a home for *bezprisorni* (homeless children) who had no-one to look after them.

'There are many there who also have no parents. You will be well looked after,' he tried to console her.

I became very frightened. If Bunchy told him I had no parents either, he might take me away as well. I hoped that this could not apply because I had Tousia. I was very upset to see Bunchy go. But what a relief! I can still remember how Bunchy clung to me and how frightened I was.

With Hanochka I had frequented nearby markets in search of food. I had seen peasant women from outlying villages standing about, muffled in their big shawls, selling potatoes, cottage cheese, milk and other produce. All the time they were on the look-out for soldiers who raided these places mercilessly in an effort to stamp out speculation. Money was worthless and fifty roubles bought only as much as ten kopeks used to buy. Peasants exchanged food only for articles of clothing or household goods. People traded in anything. Pathetic, hungry old men and women stood silently about with things no-one wanted. They were the hardest hit; even at my age I was aware of it. Occasionally a peasant moved by pity would hand them something to eat. Because hunger cannot be ignored it soon dawned on us that some of our belongings were of potential value. Scraps of silk for dressing dolls, our dolls themselves, a tablet of soap, a tablecloth, all could be traded in. Tousia rummaged through our meagre possessions but it was I who went to market in search of an advantageous exchange. I was fast developing commercial talents and my age was proving an advantage. Kind peasants felt sorry for a child and often were inclined to give me a better deal. But not always. Once I had an enormous bottle of Eau de Cologne, bearing Uncle Sacha's name on the label—a valuable commodity. It was worth at least ten pounds of potatoes or something of an equivalent value!

I stood for a moment pondering the best approach. A large, hairy *moujik* with a grin on his face and a glimmer of cupidity in his cunning little eyes spotted me.

'What have you got?' he asked. Confidently I handed him the

bottle which he proceeded to inspect. He looked so interested I was already blessing my luck. How was I to know that vodka was not always available and he was thirsty? With a sudden swift gesture he uncorked it and before I could cry out he had poured the contents in one mighty gulp down his throat. Then, laughing loudly, he handed me the empty bottle.

Upset and in tears I ran home to Tousia empty-handed. She was at pains to console me. I had not only failed miserably but I was also thoroughly humiliated and very cross at having made such a blot on my commercial reputation. That evening we ate potato peelings fried in a tiny bit of lard, our staple diet when things were grim. Many days passed before I consented to brave the market again.

This hand-to-mouth existence continued with varied and sometimes unexpected results. Once a peasant woman, tempted by an attractive tablecloth, offered me for it a large, fat, live rabbit. The opportunity was too good to miss—we had not tasted meat for weeks and the thought alone made my mouth water. Jubilant, hugging the furry beast inside my coat and feeling him against me warm and friendly, I came home. Brought up with pets, I had never faced the dilemma confronting me. How was I to kill it? Tousia and I felt like a couple of murderers planning an execution. Help came from an unexpected quarter. The area *dvornik* (janitor) knocked at the door to inform Tousia it was her turn to sweep the snow in front of the house. All were obliged to perform some sort of work and the stints even included sweeping tramlines at night. He was a kindly old man and, I think, he pitied us and wanted to help.

'A rabbit!' he said. 'You are lucky! I'll kill it for you, nothing easier,' and before we had time to acquiesce, he delivered one mighty blow on the rabbit's neck. Stunned by the rapidity of the execution, we felt close to tears. But as we picked up the lifeless body, another problem faced us. The animal had to be drawn and skinned, and for that we had first to sever the head. It was no use being squeamish. I proved the bravest. An axe for chopping wood lay under the stairs so, picking it up, I put the rabbit on the cement floor, closed my eyes and wielded the axe with all my strength.

Something hot and sticky spurted into my face. There was blood everywhere. Tousia had fainted—she could never stand the sight of blood—and the head had disappeared! It must have hit the low ceiling and ricocheted from it. When Tousia came to, we both crawled on our hands and knees trying to find it. It had wedged itself solidly behind a cupboard. We retrieved it and made soup out of it. Nothing was to be wasted. What a meal we cooked! Neither did we forget Mama. Whenever luck was with us, we shared our rations with her by taking a food parcel to the prison. (We had by now discovered she was in Boutirki Prison.)

We were not always so lucky. Once we bartered a precious possession for a sheep's head only to discover on closer examination that it was the head of a dog, and probably an old one at that. We cooked it just the same, wasting precious fuel, but the smell proved so revolting it made us both sick.

For several weeks we searched for food or devised means by which it could be obtained. Although we still tried to go to school, we went at different times and it was difficult for Tousia to keep me up to the mark. And with no Hanochka to scold, encourage or explain, I often missed a day, sometimes longer. And when I attended I did not learn much. New teachers had by now replaced the old, and they taught me a creed which, young as I was, I already hated. Although with others I sang *The Internationale* at the top of my voice, I was far more astute than my teachers thought and the party propaganda which taught us to spy on parents and denounce them made me feel sick. Loyalty would always be what I admired most because Hanochka had preached it. Besides, it was more fun being a hooligan than sitting at a desk, hunched up against a cold so intense that sometimes the ink froze.

I had also fallen in love. The object of my affections was fifteen. He terrorised everyone in his class, and when we met in the corridors he pulled my long tresses. Revolted by such treatment, I pricked up my courage and quoted an old Russian proverb, 'You chastise only those you love.' The boy with black gipsyish eyes and hair the colour of ripe corn stopped dead in his tracks, roared with laughter and from that moment we were friends. Young thieves were already nothing new to me. This young delinquent, Kolka, boasted that he had started his exploits at the age of ten after his parents disappeared. He had learned to lie, thieve and defy authority, and he pretended not to know the difference between good and evil.

'It's easier that way. I shall not die of hunger and I have no intention of being sent to an institution like your friend Bunchy.'

Although he, unlike Genia, in no way concerned himself with history, I must have felt subconsciously that events had fallen on his young head which even grown-ups were hard put to overcome and, somehow, I pitied him.

'Where do you live?' I wanted to know.

'Nowhere.'

'Do you remember your parents?'

'Very little. I only know my father used to drink and talk too much.'

'Who was he?'

'How do I know?'

Very soon under his expert guidance I was scrounging in markets, filling my pockets with stolen potatoes or carrots with no scruples whatsoever, and learning from him all the rich resources of Russian swear words. His law of the jungle was in complete contradiction to everything I had been taught, but facing this completely new world with a friend seemed much easier, and there grew a solidarity between us, an easy give and take, on which the success of our misdeeds often depended. Very soon he overstepped the mark by stealing a bundle from a very old woman whose wailing tore at my heart strings.

'Stop it, what are you doing?' I screamed in horror.

'What's the matter with you? She is older than both of us and will die before we do. Anyway, everybody steals—except Christ —and he would if his hands were not nailed to the Cross!'

Horrified by his blasphemy, I did not suspect he was only quoting an old Russian proverb.

Strangely, years later I recognised his unusual name on the programme of a Paris night club. . . . As with all bad memories, this one had effaced itself and I had no wish to resurrect it. Also, there was no reason why the stranger with the hard, disenchanted look who played the guitar to entertain the guests should have remembered me!

It was I who usually fetched a bucket of fresh snow to melt while we prepared our lessons. One evening we found the bucket also contained a large, black crow, frozen solid. We wished it had been a pigeon, as pigeon pie would have been no mean luxury. However, we were not going to waste what providence had so kindly sent us. When the bird had thawed and we had sniffed at it from all angles, we pronounced it quite fresh. How death had overtaken it remained a mystery. We were none too keen to eat it ourselves; potatoes or bread would be preferable and last longer than a poor old crow. A chicken in the open market could be exchanged very favourably for almost anything, especially if a rich commissar's wife wanted it, and this we were both astute enough to know. So Tousia proceeded to pluck it, cutting off its feet and head, and tied it up most professionally as she had seen Kirianovna do. We now had the most magnificent chicken imaginable, the taste of which we were not prepared to guarantee!

I could hardly wait to go to the market next morning! Those illegal markets were our lifeline, and although they were frequently raided, Kolka had taught me how not to be caught red-handed. The Food Commissariat constantly protested about the encroachment on its monopoly, but without it we and many others could not have survived.

I had a stroke of luck when I spotted a woman looking in my direction. I had previously noticed her buying expensive items from various peasants and I knew she was good for a valuable exchange. 'What have you got?' she asked, as she saw me unwrapping and fingering my crow.

'A beautiful, plump chicken,' I lied.

She was immediately interested.

'How much?'

The old crow, thanks to Tousia's tender ministrations, looked luscious, and she had even powdered its breast. 'Fifteen pounds of potatoes and one pound of lard,' I cheekily demanded, knowing full well it was an outrageous price. But Kolka's lessons had not been in vain.

'You must be mad, child,' she reproached me. 'I will give you five pounds of potatoes and a quarter of lard.'

'No, no,' I protested vehemently. 'There is another citizen to whom I promised this beautiful bird,' and I pretended to scan the horizon for my imaginary client.

'All right, I'll give you ten pounds of potatoes and a quarter of fat. It's not worth more.'

'I must have half a pound of fat. I know the other woman will give it,' I insisted.

She must have believed me, and she produced from a huge bag the quantities that clinched the deal.

I checked the weight at a nearby stall. I had learnt plenty since my Eau de Cologne episode. Then we hurried away in different directions.

Was it my conscience or fear of the woman's wrath which, thereafter, kept me away from this particular market? There were plenty of others, and hungry people flocked to them in search of food.

CHAPTER EIGHT

The hours drew on towards evening. I was getting used to living without Mama. It was very cold and nearly dark in the flat as I waited for Tousia to return. She had told me she would be later than usual as she was going to the French School to find out whether a certain friend was back from the country.

I longed for a hot drink, but it meant going outside to fill the bucket. Let Tousia do it when she came in, I thought. I threw myself on the bed, fully dressed, and pulled the covers over to try and get warm. My legs and feet were so painful and swollen that I could hardly walk.

I must have fallen asleep. Tousia's entry woke me. She was pale and trembling all over.

'What's happened?' Something was wrong, I could see, and as usual I feared for Mama.

'I got arrested, that's what,' she snapped, still in a state of panic. 'If it hadn't been for your Genia, I would still be at the Tcheka.'

It was as if she had poured iced water down my back. Everything was changing every minute. There was no family. People just vanished or were taken away and now I had very nearly lost my sister. Then a militiaman would come and take me away like Bunchy. I shuddered.

Tousia told me that at St Catherine's she had found guards posted at every door. It reassured her. The unruly mobs had to be controlled and she thought the guards were protecting foreign property.

'Can I go through to the Head's office?' she asked the soldier at the door.

'What for?'

'I want to find out about a friend of mine.'

'Why? Can't you do without her?'

She thought the question peculiar but she insisted: 'I must find out.'

Somewhat reluctantly the soldier opened the door and she walked down familiar corridors and past deserted classrooms. At the Head's office she knocked.

'Come in,' a voice said.

A commissar was sitting at the Head's desk, she recognised him as such easily enough. They all wore leather jackets and revolvers and looked alike. She thought nothing of it and it did not surprise her. They were everywhere nowadays and this one at least had an air of authority.

'What do you want?' he growled at her.

She explained, adding that she herself was not a pupil here. The commissar scrutinised her closely, then made an almost invisible sign to a soldier standing by the window.

'Come with me, girl,' this one said roughly.

Tousia was still not aware of any danger. She turned to obey and saw that another soldier had joined them.

'Hands behind your back, march!' he commanded, in a voice that stood no argument. In no time at all she found herself in the street, being led between two soldiers in the direction of the Tcheka. There used to be a friendly policeman at the corner who always saluted her as she went past to her catechism lessons. Most of the tradesmen in the street also knew her. But now the shutters were up, the shops were closed and the street completely deserted. The air of the Loubianka had become unhealthy to breathe. 'It struck me this was a different town, a strange town I was seeing for the first time,' she explained.

They marched in silence and it took them ten minutes to reach their destination. As they entered the dreaded building, she thought of Mama, and that she too must have crossed this threshold. Unceremoniously she was pushed into a small room and told to wait. 'I was by now trembling all over and could not control it. I longed to run away but guards were everywhere. Besides, they had locked the door on me.'

There was a makeshift bed in the room, a table and a chair. It looked as if someone slept here. The little window had bars on it. 'As I went up to it I suddenly noticed behind the flimsy curtain something I had never expected to see. A small ikon of the Virgin stood there and a little *lampada* (night light) was burning in front of it. In this unholy place someone believed!'

This discovery brought her peace, she told me. On an impulse, she knelt on the filthy floor and began to pray ... 'Mother of God, help of the afflicted' ... and as her lips moved in an unceasing litany an almost miraculous certitude that everything would be all right slowly invaded her.

A key turned in the lock.

'This way.' She drew on her newly found courage and followed the guard into a room where, sitting at a long table, several men in some sort of uniform were questioning prisoners.

She felt someone's gaze on her and, looking up, saw a young soldier standing behind one of the sitting commissars.

'My mind was so confused and the face, somehow familiar, was so drawn and tired, I almost failed to recognise him. All at once I knew. It was Genia. But the look he gave me forbade any sign.'

She watched men and women being questioned and then led away. She was sure they were not being released! Presently her turn came, a guard pushed her forward, but as she faced the commissar, Genia bent down and whispered into the ear of the one who appeared to be the leader. The man looked up, surprised, then silently nodded. A Genia she could not have imagined, so severe and rough was his manner, ordered her to follow him. Without another word and very quickly they crossed the whole building to a back door. From a bunch of keys Genia selected one which opened it and practically threw her out into the street. Not stopping to catch her breath she had run all the way home.

A feeling of overwhelming gratitude welled up inside me. Genia had helped, Genia was a friend after all, God keep him safe.

'Do you think the soldiers will come as they did after Mama's arrest?' The thought made me feel cold all over.

'Of course not. They don't even know my name, so how could they?'

'You don't think Genia will tell?'

'If he did, they would find out that he let me go and they would shoot him, wouldn't they?'

This seemed logical, but all the same I was not fully reassured. Life was becoming increasingly frightening. I put my arms around Tousia and held her tight. She was my little mother now and I was so afraid to lose her.

For a few seconds we clung to each other. Then, disengaging herself from my embrace, she rummaged around and produced a few frozen potatoes, grey and sour, which she mashed up and made into croquettes by pouring boiling water over them. I made the tea and we drank it with the remainder of some sugar. Our larder was quite empty and we had nothing else to barter.

'Tomorrow we shall have to see Kousmich,' Tousia decided.

Papa had left a lot of money with Kousmich in case of emergencies. We had no option but to contact him and ask for help. Besides, we were both very anxious to let him know how splendidly his son had behaved, in spite of all his revolutionary zeal. I would go with Tousia, I refused to let her out of my sight, especially as at the factory there were armed guards on duty whom we considered to be our enemies, although the workers were our friends.

'If they arrest you, they'll have to take me too,' I kept repeating, determined not to be separated.

We were relieved to see the gates of the factory unguarded. Discipline was lax and everyone was his own master at that time, at least the proletariat thought so! The guard had probably gone to have tea. Kousmich, in his usual workshop, was alarmed to see us. Luckily there was no-one about. Hurriedly, in a few words, Tousia explained our predicament and told him about Genia. The old man listened silently, looking at us with great sadness. His eyes conveyed plainer than any words that he was wondering when his country would come to its senses. He promised to come after work and bring some money. The sum mentioned was so small that Tousia indignantly protested.

'But Kousmich, how do you expect us to manage on such a pittance?'

'The *barine* gave me what he did because he trusted me and only to the *barine* will I give it back,' Kousmich replied, a stubborn look crossing his face. No further entreaties or mild threats could accomplish anything. Papa had judged Kousmich at his right value. The old man had his own code of honour which nothing could shift, so all we could do was to accept his help. Times were hard, everyone had to scrape and pinch, but secretly we admired Kousmich because his own family went even hungrier than we did.

Mama had many admirers, one of the most assiduous beign

Alexis, a Russian friend of Papa's and, at one time, a frequent guest at our house. Of course I was not able to assess her attitude towards him which, at times, appeared oddly unsympathetic and impatient, but Papa enjoyed his company and was always gay in his presence. Of old merchant stock, Alexis' commercial dealings were with England, a country he frequently visited. A confirmed Anglophile, his admiration for that country knew no bounds. He even sent his shirts to be washed and ironed in London and was always criticising an aunt of his who lived there because she sent her blouses to France for the same purpose! Invariably when he came to see us he brought me some exotic toy or a large box of chocolates and the glamour of distant places hung around him. After receiving his present, I would retire to my nursery and laboriously write him a thank-you letter, enclosing a small photograph of myself with my favourite teddy bear. This was a ritual which never varied and I spent a lot of kopeks on passport photos!

When I was about four and ready for bed one evening, I caught sight of myself in the mirror. The reflection of a little girl in a long, white nightie with black, shiny hair almost down to the ground must have pleased me or else I was already becoming a real daughter of Eve.

'Hanochka,' I begged, 'please ask Alexis to come and say goodnight to me.'

My request was not unusual. He often strolled into my bedroom when dining with my parents and sometimes lingered on to tell me some wonderful story, fact, fiction or legend, but equally entrancing. The only difference this time was that it was I who asked him.

'My, my, so you want me to see how pretty you look tonight!' he exclaimed, smiling broadly.

Profoundly humiliated that he should have seen through me, I disappeared under my bedclothes.

'Go away,' I screamed, 'I don't want you.'

Alexis had been best man at my parents' wedding and, he unashamedly declared, on that day he had first set eyes on Mama and fallen in love with her. I certainly believed him because Mama could and did arouse great devotion in those around her.

'That is why I have remained a bachelor ever since!' he would add and Papa would laugh and smilingly infer that in reality nothing had any hold on him and he enjoyed being free. But I found Alexis' story beautifully romantic. When he remained absent for long stretches, I inquired as to his whereabouts. That his connections were wide and mysterious was obvious even to me and after the outbreak of the revolution I often heard grownups discuss how he kept out of all involvement with the new government—apparently a rare achievement.

'He always knows whose paw he must grease,' Papa commented.

To me he was some sort of magician.

'I wish Alexis would come back,' Tousia suddenly volunteered. 'He would know what to do.'

As if in answer to our prayers, a week later he was back in Moscow and soon traced us to our wretched hovel. Shocked to see us swollen from cold and hunger, he moved us into a warm apartment in a house he still owned. His old *niania* was ordered to look after us and get us back into shape, with all the necessities of life miraculously provided.

'You are not to worry about anything, girls!' he assured us. 'I will see that your mother is returned to you and meantime you must both attend school regularly.'

He put a stop to all my activities on the black market.

'It's lucky I found you when I did. You are not yet past redeeming!' he told me.

Under Niania's supervision regular life was restarted and a certain sense of security returned, except that we missed our parents. Somehow Mama's imprisonment seemed more dreadful than Papa's. I think it was the shock of finding out how people you loved could disappear into thin air. Alexis came daily and kept a watchful eye on our well-being. He was trying to find out where and how Mama had been arrested and what the charges against her were. He interviewed endless commissars but made little progress. Occasionally he confided to us his discouragement. Three months went by while we hoped, prayed and waited.

Then, looking preoccupied and gloomy, 'Children,' he said, 'you must be prepared for bad news. The authorities are not ready to let your mother go. I have finally established what the charge is. She is accused of speculating, and that is serious!'

'How could she, in prison?' I asked. The word held no secrets for me.

'They say she sold liquor to the troops to get them drunk and

94

make them disobey orders, when you were still in your own house.'

'But that's ridiculous.'

'I know, I know.' Alexis tried to soothe us. 'It's all lies but nevertheless the accusation is very serious and you must be brave.'

Then he went into details of how the charge arose. Unruly soldiers had roamed the streets looking for the cellars of rich householders in order to get drunk. In our place they discovered a real Aladdin's cave full of imported French wines which they had never tasted before. They found them to their liking and next morning were found sprawling all over the factory grounds. Our own indignant workers reported the orgy to the authorities, and now they had found nothing better than to pin this accusation on Mama!

The implication of Alexis' words was not lost on us. We knew such a charge could carry the death penalty. Young as we were, we were fully conversant with revolutionary horrors and the prospect dazed us.

'I am negotiating with a very highly placed government official,' said Alexis, 'so I must go. It is important I keep in touch with him as by tomorrow the situation will be resolved—one way or another.'

A twinge of fear went through me. I did not dare to look at Tousia in case she guessed what ran through my head. Yet, because of the close link between us, our thoughts must have been identical. The execution, if it was to take place, would be tonight!

'How could they do anything to her?' Tousia moaned. 'They have not dared touch a foreigner until now.'

Alexis nodded. 'Yes, this is exactly the line I am taking with the official. I have also offered a large ransom, so cheer up, girls, we mustn't lose hope,' he added.

But my heart had turned to ice. I could not take the situation in. Savage cruelties I understood, but death for someone so near was altogether beyond my imagination. Yet the thought that Mama might be shot kept coming back. I remembered wondering whether she would ever return? I looked at Tousia. Wise beyond her years, she sat there with weary resignation. After Alexis left, Niania fussed over us with unaccustomed tenderness but we scarcely touched the food she placed in front of us and we hardly spoke. At last, worn out, I fell asleep in Tousia's arms and dreamt she was in truth my little mother.

But the worst did not happen and things continued as before. What we would have done without Alexis, I cannot think. At that time there was no-one else to whom we could turn. It seemed incredible when he announced: 'Girls, your mother is coming home tomorrow.'

He was entirely confident that his negotiations had at last succeeded and she would be released.

Happy and excited I spent all night looking at the clock and thinking the morning would never come. At first light, the door opened and a dirty beggarwoman stood in the room calling my name. I recognised the voice and threw myself into Mama's arms. But recovering from my emotions it seemed I was kissing a stranger. Gone was the familiar fragrance of *Quelques Fleurs* I always associated with her. Instead, a strong odour of carbolic was mixed with the awful smell of destitution and the particularly insupportable odour of unwashed flesh.

'You must burn my clothes, they have not left my body for seven months,' was almost the first thing she said as she disentangled herself from our embraces. Tousia and I followed her into the bathroom where, as she stripped, we threw her filthy rags into the burning stove Niania had lit to heat the water. We helped to rub and scrub her body, which was covered with sores and bites from bugs and lice. We laced the bath water with disinfectant, washed her hair and threw more clean water over her but the peculiar prison odour stayed and would not shift for several days. But at thirty-eight she was resilient, and very soon Mama was her old courageous, indomitable self as she started planning for the future. And the future now meant getting out of Russia.

CHAPTER NINE

It was Mama herself who told us about her arrest. That morning at Lamanova's Couture Establishment she had found the shutters up and the place deserted. Lamanova lived around the corner and a pleasant young man opened the door when she knocked. Inside she saw another man and sensed danger at once. But it was too late to retreat.

'I am Koudriaftzeff, special agent of the Tcheka. Please state who you are,' he said.

Still thinking she had nothing to fear, Mama gave her name.

'Aha, a capitalist and a foreigner! Well, what have you got, money, jewelry? You had better declare it! You are under arrest and you will be searched.'

'I am hiding nothing and I am French by nationality,' she replied, still thinking there must be some mistake. The situation was too preposterous. ('I wondered,' she went on, 'where Lamanova was, and whether this was supposed to be an ambush? I also knew that the Tcheka had quite a reputation for corruption and bribery and I wondered if I should perhaps offer a bribe? But Koudriaftzeff did not look that sort of man and I was afraid to incriminate myself.')

A woman warder now appeared from nowhere and searched her. Then she locked the door and left.

'I do not remember how long I sat and waited. I was confused and wondering how I could let you know.'

'As soon as Tania told us about the strange man in the cab with you we were sure you had been arrested,' Tousia said.

'I shall never forget that first night at the Tcheka,' Mama continued. 'I was put into a cell with about forty other women. The stench was awful and came from an open latrine in the middle of the room. The women crowded around me asking who I was and why I had been arrested. But I had been warned that all prisons were infiltrated by informers and I was careful in my

97

answers. You see, I still believed they would release me after a few hours.'

'We waited for you all night,' I said. 'When did they question you, Mama?'

'They never did. It seemed as if they had forgotten all about me.'

'Mama, why did you say you would never forget the Loubianka?'

'Because of what I saw, my darling.' I remember she took first me, then Tousia in her arms and held us tight, as we both waited for her to continue. Only Niania, who had been listening, kept shaking her head in disapproval.

'They must be told, Niania,' Mama insisted.

'Every night, for the ten days I was there,' she said, 'as soon as it was dark a jailer would start calling out names at regular intervals. A prisoner whose name was called just crossed herself and left. Only rarely did one come back from what the others described as "questioning". At first I could not believe that people were being shot. But then I saw it for myself through a small gap in the window. Every night those terrible murders went on. I wondered whether my turn would come too.'

She then told us how those shootings always stopped at about 2am. 'Even assassins had to sleep.' The naked bodies were then loaded into special lorries and taken to some woods outside the town to be thrown into a previously dug common grave. The clothes of the victims were distributed, she was told, among the executioners.

'I shall never know how many Crucifixions took place every night, without the consolation of the Resurrection. No cross will ever mark the spot where someone's loved one lies. Complete obliteration, no possible identification—ever! When you think that before even a pauper had the sacred right to a coffin. Now these poor victims are only good to manure the land!'

We remained silent and dreadfully upset.

Then she talked about her transfer to the Boutirki prison, where they led them like a herd of cattle through the streets of Moscow. Although conditions there were just as bad, some of the fear at least had been removed, she said.

'Did you ever manage to communicate with Papa and Uncle Paul?' we asked.

98

Mama shook her head.

'We were fifteen women in a cell meant for four,' she continued 'and there was not an inch to spare. The cell stank abominably. There was no ventilation and the only fresh air came in when the jailer brought the food.'

'What was the food like?' Tousia asked.

Mama smiled. 'As meagre and as filthy as before. Soup made of dry fish heads (*vobla*) with a few human hairs floating in it, and a piece of black bread. But your parcels helped,' she added, seeing our crestfallen faces.

'Three times a day we were taken to the toilets under guard. This was my only exercise. There were no locks on any of the doors so if you took longer than expected, a guard intruded on your privacy. The degradation was complete.'

'But Mama, when were you finally questioned?' I asked.

'I never was, darling.'

'How did you know that you were free?' I said, uncomprehending.

'After seven months in that hell, on a morning that promised to be like any other, a guard appeared and called my name for the very first time. You can imagine how I felt! From sheer fright, my legs turned to jelly and practically refused to carry me. I followed him out of the cell. "You are free to go, citizen," he said.'

When Mama had sufficiently recovered, Kousmich came one evening after dark with the parcel Papa had entrusted to him hidden under his coat. It contained a large amount of gold, a diamond necklace, a pair of diamond ear-rings and other jewelry which had been in the house on the night all safes were requisitioned. The old man was very nervous. Genia was a revolutionary, a trusted member of the Party, and already the deadly wave of betrayals was making its appearance. Search parties broke into people's homes indiscriminately enough, God knows! The slightest suspicion or denunciation and even Kousmich's modest dwelling would not be exempt from such a visit, nor he from the punishment, if such a parcel were found, for the accomplices of capitalists—foreign ones at that.

Kousmich, cap in hand, stood in the middle of the room and lamented to Mama.

'*Barinia*, what terrible times! You can't even trust your own kin! What's to become of us all?'

'Don't worry, Kousmich, it will be all right' Mama consoled him.

'There is no end to their wickedness, *barinia*', Kousmich went on. 'They have been after Sophie and have taken away her ration cards and savings.'

'For God's sake, what has she done?' Mama cried out.

Sophie was the factory midwife. Her very first job had been with my paternal grandmother, with whom she travelled when the latter was pregnant, to replace the often panic-stricken *femme de chambre*. She had brought all of our family's children into the world as well as countless workers' children and she was loved and respected by all. Just before the revolution she retired to a cosy little house in the factory compound where we all visited her. Here she was peacefully enjoying the last years of her life. Like any old person, she adapted with difficulty to new ideas and her eternal grumblings could sometimes seem perilously close to insolence. And so it came about that some over-zealous party member had denounced this counter-revolutionary of eighty-four to the authorities with the disastrous results Kousmich was relating to Mama.

'You must help her, *barinia*,' he pleaded, tears streaming in rivulets down his cheeks.

Mama did, with food and money, for as long as we remained in Moscow. Sophie's ultimate fate we were never able to discover. It was pathetic how many of those old, simple folk relied on my parents who, by now, could do very little.

In the apartment above ours lived a fairly well-known actor with whom we shared the attic. Actors enjoyed a large degree of immunity and because of it the attic was not likely to be searched. As for the man himself, Mama and Alexis had reservations and were inclined to distrust him.

One evening, when he was out, we crept upstairs and hid the jewelry Kousmich had returned under the floorboards in various places. We then replaced everything as before and left no sign of our intrusion.

Mama breathed easier and we resumed our respective chores. The most important was to track down food, to provide for ourselves, our two prisoners and whoever else Mama felt under an obligation to help. We had found a black-market trader in horse-flesh, and now that we could pay in gold we became his

A group of the factory's female workers in 1891

Religious services were frequently held at the factory

The entrance to the Moscow house through the winter garden, 1890.
Claude Giraud is seated, Victor is standing in the centre

The family's country house, Himki

best customers. All other meat had long ago disappeared. Dogs, cats, pigeons and other domestic animals were nowhere to be seen. Horse-flesh, if it was young and healthy, was quite delicious. Of course the same could not be claimed of an old nag, in which case the smell was often so strong that no disguise did anything. 'Russian cutlets' were made by mincing any sinewy flesh, adding potato peelings or a crust of bread, seasoning it well—at one time salt was unobtainable—and cooking it. We had become experts at culinary camouflage! It was most important that Papa and Uncle Paul did not recognise the food we sent them for what it was. The latter had declared many times that he would never, never touch horse-flesh—come what may. Locked up in prison for a year, he could not know to what we had been reduced.

Extraordinary as it may seem, the one commodity never in short supply was money. Where it came from in such vast amounts once Mama was out of prison I do not know, and sadly I think of all the questions I have left unasked. There is no-one to enlighten me now. All I remember is that money resembled wallpaper and Mama used to cut large sheets of it with a pair of tailor's scissors. It was worth very little. Sometimes she entrusted me with a school satchel full of it to take to some address. A child was less likely to be stopped and searched. I hurried away with a sense of tremendous importance and hundreds of butter-flies in my tummy. There were so many secrets I had learned to keep and it was difficult to sort out which were the most impor-tant. When dear Uncle Paul's first and characteristic gesture on reaching Paris was to present Tousia and me with identical pearl necklaces, 'as a reward,' he said, 'for never having fed me disgusting horse-flesh,' there could thereafter never be any question of confessing the truth.

In the atmosphere of suspense and uncertainty, always waiting for something to happen, search-parties were a regular feature. 'We are looking for arms and ammunition,' the soldiers pro-claimed as they burst in, but it was only an excuse for taking anything they wanted and often, if something failed to take their fancy, they just wantonly destroyed it, turning the place upside down. We spent our time tidying up!

Once, Mama was rummaging through a tin box, sorting out what else to barter. A peasant had promised to bring some produce. Suddenly there was the dreaded knock at the door which we never failed to recognise because it was made with the butt of a gun. It must have been early spring. The window behind me was open and gave on to a garden gone to rack and ruin because whoever it had belonged to no longer claimed ownership nor tended it. In the next few seconds everything happened at once. Tousia jumped towards the door to shield us, and at the same moment Mama pushed the small box towards me. That was enough. I snatched it, jumped out of the window and raced across the waste ground with no aim in mind, in a purely reflex action to run away as far as possible. Almost immediately I realised I was being pursued. One of the soldiers must have spotted me in spite of Tousia's delaying action.

'Oh God, let me escape!' I prayed as I reached a familiar cluster of thick bushes. The day before I had seen a thrush returning to feed its young, but the nest was so well concealed I had spent a long time finding it. Now a sudden inspiration made me plunge into the maze and stuff the box alongside the nest among the branches. The disturbed bird squawked loudly in protest as it flew off while, extricating myself, I continued to run. I was out of breath, slowing down and all the time searching in my head for a likely story to tell the man who, I knew, was about to catch me.

'Stop at once!' his gruff voice ordered, and I obeyed.

'Why did you run away?' he asked.

'I was just scared,' I whispered and felt a cramp in my stomach.

'Scared of what?' He looked at me suspiciously, then passed his hands over my pockets and turned me round, examining me. 'Are you hiding anything?' he asked.

I shook my head. 'We have nothing left,' I replied, and remembered to look pathetic.

'Why run away then, we are not going to eat you?'

'I am afraid of soldiers, some of them are not very nice,' I stuttered lamely, at a loss to find a better explanation.

'We won't hurt you. We are only obeying orders, searching rich bourgeois like you. Are you sure your mother is not hiding anything?'

He looked at me searchingly when I said no. Then he led me back. Mama was at the window and I saw her anxious eyes. I smiled reassuringly and she must have realised the box had disappeared. The soldiers left having found nothing. I rushed back into the garden. The thrush was back in its nest and this time I retrieved the box very gently so as not to disturb it. I felt very grateful towards it, because in its own humble way it had helped me, and very proud of myself as I handed the box back to Mama.

It was soon after this episode that Alexis moved in with us. It was his house, he had looked after Tousia and me and had been instrumental in returning Mama to us. With Papa in prison, he was a welcome protector and life was decidedly easier when he was around. That summer food had become so scarce, even he with all his extraordinary connections could not always obtain it. Peasants were reluctant to bring their produce to town because trains were constantly raided and the food ruthlessly confiscated. The peasants themselves were liable to be carried off to prison and, in bad cases, shot. The government was taking draconian measures.

So when I opened the door to a peasant woman of enormous proportions, I was somewhat taken aback.

'What do you want?' Alexis asked.

'I have come to deliver your order, *barine*,' she answered.

'But where is it?' He obviously did not recognise the woman.

'Hidden on my person, *barine*,' she replied. 'Just you be patient', and a few seconds later she laid out on the table a large side of pork, flour, butter, cheese and even eggs—all completely unobtainable in Moscow. She herself, to my amazement, was now as thin as a rake!

But there were other less fortunate episodes. A bearded stranger we had never seen before knocked at the door one night, offering a forty-pound sack of flour. This was indeed lucky, we had been without bread for days. Kirianovna, pottering about, helped to inspect the flour which appeared of particularly fine quality, unusually free from adulteration. The sack was checked for weight on the kitchen scales, and the man was paid. He seemed in a great hurry and very nervous, which was attributed to the fact he had never called before.

'You'd better weigh up five pounds for yourself, Kirianovna, and put the rest into tins so the rats don't get at it,' Mama recommended. As Kirianovna started to do this, from an adjoining room we heard her gasp and invoke the deity and all the saints. She was prostrating herself in the corner where, by decree, no ikons were any longer allowed to hang. In her distress she had forgotten it and acted out of sheer habit. An unrecognisable object lay on the floor, smothered in flour. Mama's eagle-eye must have caught sight of it and I was immediately ordered out. I could not fathom out why . . . There continued to be a lot of activity and whisperings behind the door and strange remarks . . . 'It would have been much easier to put a stone in it . . . What shall we do? How dreadful . . .'

Something very unusual had happened, something frightening, otherwise Kirianovna would not have been so upset, but what? I was left to guess. Shourka, who had come to visit, was sent to fetch Philipoch. After I had gone to bed, I heard footsteps outside. I pressed my nose to the window pane and saw Alexis and Philipoch carrying a sack and spades. But the night was dark and I could see nothing more. The incident was not referred to again, at least not in my presence and I forgot about it until a few weeks later, when Shourka, who these days always seemed to have some secret to impart, suddenly volunteered that there was a baby buried in the garden.

'What baby?' I demanded.

'The one that was brought in the bag of flour.'

My curiosity was aroused and I pressed Shourka for an explanation.

'He was dead when Kirianovna found him. He was put into the sack to make it heavier. A whole ten pounds more, my mother said.'

'Whose was it?' I wanted to know.

'How do I know?' Shourka disdainfully replied and dismissed the whole affair. She was getting above herself, I thought. All that because she was sixteen and some commissar was chasing after her!

CHAPTER TEN

Almost a year had elapsed since Papa and Uncle Paul had been
arrested. A pass to visit them had at last been granted. How had
they weathered those long, weary months when Papa had not
known that, at one time, Mama had shared the same address with
him in Boutirki prison? There had been no direct communication and we were not even sure that our food parcels reached
them regularly.

At the gates of the Andronevsky Monastery we queued,
showed our passes which stated in what capacity and whom we
had come to visit, and then waited with a dozen or so people
assembled no doubt for the same purpose. I noticed a young
woman holding a very tiny, puny baby, newly born, standing
slightly apart. She looked pathetic and forlorn as she held the
child close to herself as if trying to warm it. After some time we
were admitted into an empty courtyard. Strong, stone walls
surrounded it. I was not to know then that, according to Soljenitzin, Andronevsky Monastery was the first concentration
camp the Russians had devised. I only thought of it as a grim
prison.

We stood around in the intense cold for about ten minutes.
Then gates leading to the inner part opened and about a dozen
men stormed out. Almost at once I was lifted into Papa's arms
and he was hugging and kissing me. Mother's and Tousia's turn
came next, while I looked around for Uncle Paul. To my great
surprise I saw the young woman I had spotted hand the baby to
him and the next moment, with an ecstatic look of happiness, he
rushed with it towards Mama.

'Look at him, Liouba,' he cried, 'look at my wonderful baby
son!' and, handing her the baby, embraced us all tenderly.

I was very puzzled.

'Verochka,' he commanded, 'come here.' The young woman
advanced shyly, shook hands with my parents, smiled at me and

was led away by my uncle to a quiet corner where, with his arm wrapped protectively around her and the baby, they were presently absorbed in deep conversation. It had seemed to me my parents had been slightly embarrassed by the incident, but they were now busily discussing the events of the last year—a lot had to be said in the forty-five minutes the visit was to last.

I wondered who the mysterious Verochka was and why I had neither seen nor heard of her before? Why did Uncle Paul call the tiny tot his son? Had Aunt Isabelle left a baby behind and, if so, why was he not living with us? I lost myself completely in conjectures. When the time came to part, Papa hugged me so tightly I thought he would never let me go. I felt uncomfortable. The guards were hurrying our goodbyes and Verochka, clinging to my uncle, was sobbing without any restraint. I had never witnessed such a demonstrative scene before, and I could see Papa and Mama were trying to ignore it.

The minute we were outside the prison walls, I asked, 'Who is Verochka, Mama?' I wanted to know. But unexpectedly Mama looked very cross and evasive.

'Don't ask so many questions, child,' she snapped. I looked at Tousia, but she too was non-committal.

At home I heard Mama discuss the visit with Alexis. Suddenly he raised his voice: 'But this is ridiculous. He'll never be able to take her out of Russia. I told him so at the very beginning. The man is besotted but it is unfair for him to raise her hopes.'

Then more incomprehensible mumbo-jumbo while I pretended to be absorbed in my algebra.

'What a tragedy for her! Such a young girl!' It was Mama again. 'He has wanted a son so badly these last few years. It is a dreadful business—probably a punishment for the way he has treated his own son.'

Decidedly, I could not make any sense out of their conversation. Why must they speak in riddles? It had been the same when Mama and Hanochka had discussed Aunt Isabelle's departure. They had exchanged meaningful glances and shaken their heads, murmuring accusingly: 'She should have stayed behind and let the children go with the governesses. No good will come of leaving a man to his own devices at a time like this. She is asking for trouble.'

Tousia and I adored our Uncle Paul and his particularly potent

108

charm and magnetism also appealed to Mama, in whom he used to confide. To Mama he recounted his various peccadilloes although, on the whole, Mama later told me, he was at heart a good family man. Apparently when he strayed from the straight and narrow, he did so with ugly women only, saying that at night all cats are black.

'You see, Liouba, to court a beautiful woman takes too much time and patience, neither of which I possess. I have to send flowers, pay compliments, prepare the stage. Whereas if I only glance at an ugly one, she is so grateful for male attention, she is ready to jump into bed at once.'

After his tragic death Mama often spoke to me about him.

When his family had left for France this gregarious man in his early forties, who had always unashamedly enjoyed the good things in life, felt forsaken. In one mighty blow he had been deprived of his wife and children, most of his friends, his business and his properties, and now he had time on his hands. On some train journey he met a girl with nothing much to recommend her except her youth—she was only twenty-two, and her freshness appealed to him. Verochka, the daughter of a minor rail employee, had been in the habit of attending communist meetings with her father and thought of the wealthy classes as tyrants and blood suckers. The rew régime was busy preaching class hatred to the proletariat. As she confided to him all her utopian theories, he listened greatly amused. They arranged to meet again. Soon he fell head over heels in love and his worldly charm swept her off her feet. She discovered with stupefaction how completely contrary to her ideas this particular capitalist was. She began to wish the revolution had never taken place.

She was too naïve to understand that in normal times their romance could not have happened and that, in any case, now it could have no future. Their association lasted two months but it is not time that makes a passion strong. When Uncle Paul was arrested, Verochka discovered she was with child. Free love was being firmly preached by the new régime, yet her proletarian family ostracised her. Friends of my uncle, Alexis among them, managed to keep her going through the difficult months, and eventually a boy was born, a weak, undernourished child. This was the baby I had seen. One can only guess the plans and problems of their unsettled lives which they discussed that day in the prison courtyard. How could they have imagined it was to be their final meeting and that neither would ever know the fate that befell the other.

Olga Vasilievna, the mother of Tania and Lera, was Mama's friend. She had owned a small *dacha* near Moscow. It had been requisitioned in 1917 and looted several times but it had been empty ever since. Famine was so acute in Moscow that the two mothers decided that summer to send us there. The two eldest could look after the youngsters, and surely there was more likelihood of finding milk and vegetables in the country. Besides, all sorts of epidemics were raging in Moscow.

We were packed off to Lianosovo each with a small suitcase containing a bag of rice, a goosefeather cushion, an ikon and a few requisites. We were all four dreadfully thin and our mothers were worried by our pale and hungry faces. They thought it a wise decision and promised to visit us in turn, every few days.

At Lianosovo, opening the house with the keys which Olga Vasilievna had kept presented no problem, but we found the place so deserted as to be eerie. The garden was so overgrown that branches had grown into the shutters and we had to break them off before we could open up. As usual, we disturbed a family of rats. We were fully accustomed to these animals taking over wherever they could. The shambles did not dismay us, we were children of the revolution. We tidied up, arranged what there was as best we could and made our beds as comfortable as possible.

In the nearby village a peasant agreed to sell us as much skimmed milk as we wanted—for a consideration. The rest he fed to his pigs. Soon we found out that the skimmed milk was further diluted with water, so his pigs did not go short. We boiled the rice in this liquid and ate it as one would soup, as long as our stocks lasted. Often it did not assuage our young appetites, which the country air tended to stimulate. Tousia and Tania were heroic but with the selfishness of young children we appreciated it only much later. Because we were the youngest they sacrificed to us half of their portions but in spite of such abnegation we often could not fall asleep because of the clamorous hunger in our bellies. But our mothers insisted we were at least keeping out of mischief and breathing plenty of unpolluted air!

We tried new experiments to assuage our hunger with all kinds of roots. We picked sorrel and stinging nettles to make soup, but the main ingredients were missing. Prowling for food along a path behind some peasant huts, I saw a hen sitting in a hedge. I hid and waited to see if she was laying an egg. After a minute or two she started clucking joyously, so I promptly threw a stone at her, dived into the hedge and retrieved a lovely brown egg— surely God's gift for my patience! For the next four or five days I returned to the same spot and so did the hen, and every evening a hard-boiled egg was divided into four portions. Then something went amiss and the hen disappeared, but now Lera came to the rescue. There was a large quantity of blotting paper in one of the cupboards, at which the rats had had a go. Doing her homework, hungry as usual, she wondered whether those filthy animals had found a new source of food of which we were unaware.

'If the rats can eat it, why can't we?' she thought, and proceeded to put the theory into practice. The first piece tasted of nothing, but she persevered and had a second go, then drank a glass of water. Was her hunger less acute or was it her imagination? She rolled the blotting paper into little nuggets and swallowed a few with more water. She definitely felt better! Elated, she let me into her secret and I was only too happy to follow suit. Swallow and drink, swallow and drink, for the first time in weeks my stomach felt full. Joyfully we shared the discovery with our big sisters, but they doubted us until one of them tumbled to the fact that blotting paper, mixed with water, could act as sponge and swell in our insides. If it had no nourishment, at least it did give us a strong illusion and we welcomed it as a real godsend to supplement our rations.

We were becoming bored with country life. Familiar with the muddle and disturbances of town life, there were too many days in the country when nothing happened. In Moscow, between going to school, queuing for food and scrounging or simply playing truant with no-one to keep me in check, I had taken things as they came, finding funny sides to them and certainly not regretting the loss of our former life of riches and comfort, which to me spelled discipline. Adversity did not mean much and so long as the discomforts were not too acute, there was no misfortune in our new life. On the contrary, it was a challenge. It was difficult to think back and realise in what luxury we had lived; sometimes I even wondered whether it had all been a dream. Anyway, I did not spend any time dwelling on the past. It had been my parents' world and I was not destined to live like that.

Quite by chance we stumbled on the idea of walking to our old country home in Himki and effecting a food raid there. Why not? Cross country it only lay about 10 miles away. On some old map the two big sisters traced the route to take, mostly through woods and swamps, which was frighteningly exciting. Next day we started in the cool of the morning. Tania and Tousia were going barefoot—to save shoe-leather was essential—so we two youngsters, always eager to emulate our elders, did the same. Our enthusiasm carried us on for the first few kilometres, but after that the sun rose and it became quite hot even in the woods. Lera felt tired and my feet were sore. Badly damaged during the winter, they had not healed properly. So we lagged behind and finally refused to go any further, squatted under a tree and fell asleep. By the time I woke up, the sun had gone down and the swelling on my feet had subsided.

Meanwhile Tousia had prospected and now triumphantly announced that we were only about four kilometres from Himki. Revived by the hope of what we might find in our old place where every nook and cranny was so well known to us, we plodded on. Unfortunately, before long, our bare feet started sinking into squelching marshy ground, so we had to retrace our steps and find another path. This took us through forest so dense and bracken which scratched so mercilessly that we wished we had never started. We were afraid of being caught in it at night. At last the trees became sparser and the light increased. We emerged into a meadow and recognised in the distance the familiar outline of our mill. It renewed my energy as I began to think of the grain we would scoop, the mushrooms I would pick in my favourite haunts and the fruit and vegetables with which we would fill our sacks. Not to mention the delicious meal all these delicacies would produce . . . With childlike inconsistency I was seeing familiar landscapes as they used to be—my enthusiasm made me forget all that had happened.

The reality was quite different. The place was deserted and even unfriendly, abandoned and forlorn. Where were the people who had worked on the estate and who had been my friends?

The past had vanished—a hurricane had swept through. The ornamental statues in the front garden were smashed to smithereens and only fragments of white marble lay in the overgrown grass. No flower beds or paths were any longer discernible. After only three years it was all an untidy waste ground where there had been so much beauty before. Around me everything was sadly decaying. I fought my way through a litter of fallen branches to the banks of the lake where whole trees had fallen in and were rotting. Elsewhere reeds had taken possession and made access difficult. The water too was filthy, with a lot of rubbish floating in it.

Saddened and silent we wandered about, then went back to the house. Some of the shutters were open but there was no-one about. We tried one of the doors, then another—all were locked. I peeped into the windows of what had been Mama's bedroom. A couple of broken chairs and a smashed mirror lay in the middle. The room had been thoroughly turned over, even the wallpaper had been torn off.

'Why did they take it away from us if they don't want it?' I thought, but my question remained unanswered. We were probably all thinking alike.

The desolation continued wherever we looked. The stables were empty, the granary was burnt down, the *manège* partly destroyed. I went alone to the hut that had been used by Lukeria, the poultrywoman. This too was in ruins. I sat on the stump of a felled tree and memories came back. I saw myself creeping into her hut, unseen by Hanochka. A multitude of newly hatched chicks were running all over the floor. Lukeria loved her birds and talked to them. She scorned all modern methods, despised the latest incubators and reared chicks her own way and most successfully at that! There were always broody hens sitting in wooden cases under her bed.

'They like it that way,' she would confide. 'It is dark and warm and they are not disturbed.'

After the eggs had hatched, the little balls of yellow fluff were allowed the complete freedom of her hut and Lukeria transformed herself into a real mother hen while the birds which had served their purpose were, rather cruelly I thought, relegated to the chicken runs. I gathered stinging nettles with her or rather watched her do it, for she seemed immune to their stings. She then chopped these up, mixing them with cooked millet and hard-boiled eggs. As we sat on the floor she showed me how, by tapping a finger on the bare wooden boards, I could teach the baby chicks to peck. She also philosophised on the mysteries and troubles in her yard which were all attributed to the evil eye. The latter, it seems, could enter your body when you yawned, so when she yawned she never failed to make the sign of the cross over her mouth to keep it out! Now she too had gone, with so much else that I had known.

I walked towards the gardener's cottage and, miracle of miracles, it was solidly barricaded as if someone was coming back. But in the overgrown vegetable garden I only found a few carrots among the weeds and a few green plums still hung on the orchard trees. Our long trek had been in vain, but we were scared to return as night was falling, and we decided to sleep here, in the familiar house. Without any compunction whatsoever, we smashed a window and climbed in. Inside we failed to find anything to sleep on other than the bare floorboards.

For a long time I tried to find a comfortable position. Suddenly, I was on the shores of the lake with Papa and Matvei, our giant coachman who sometimes acted as a sort of gillie. Nets had just been hauled in and were full of shiny silver fish and extraordinary water creatures. Fascinated, I watched Matvei's enormous paws transfer the miraculous catch into countless buckets lined up along the bank as Papa urged him on. 'Go on, Matvei, have a go!' At which command Matvei picked up the largest fish by its tail and gulped it down, head first, and I could see it swimming round and round in his tummy which had become a large aquarium. 'Please swallow some little ones, Matvei!' I begged, as I hopped around him while he flashed his sparkling white teeth which, Kirianovna had told me, were polished so bright by the black bread he always chewed.

I woke up with a start. My right arm had gone to sleep and the pins and needles in it were excruciating. But Matvei really had existed, and he had often swallowed live fish! In fact, he had greatly appreciated such a delicacy! How I wished I had also dreamt of Lukeria. Where were they now, all those lovable, maddening, pathetically funny types? I longed for them as I tossed and turned, and listened to the old house creaking. Was it also moaning for its old inhabitants, I wondered?

A few days after we had returned to Lianosovo, Tania developed a sore throat and a high temperature. Next day she was worse and the village doctor diagnosed scarlet fever. Olga Vasilievna, whose turn it was to visit, took us all back to Moscow. Lianosovo had not proved as successful as our mothers had hoped although, except for Tania, it had restored colour to our faded cheeks. But Tania's condition grew quickly worse. A couple of days later, she had a slight haemorrhage and, towards the evening, her temperature rose alarmingly. All that night Olga Vasilievna was by her daughter's bedside. In the morning, she told Mama, Tania's breathing seemed a little easier, her face was serene and her lips were smiling; but when the doctor came and put his hand over her heart, he pronounced her dead. Because of the fear of infection none of us were allowed to see her and neither did we attend her funeral. After Tania's death Lera grew closer to us and she and I soon became inseparable. She missed her big sister dreadfully.

Coming home from school some time in late September, we saw a long queue on the corner of a nearby street. We soon discovered there had been a delivery of fish and so joined other hopefuls. It was an accepted dictum never to miss an opportunity of obtaining food. About an hour and a half later, when I handed the fish to Tousia in the kitchen, she spotted a strange insect on the side of my neck. We both knew that to catch typhus, then at its peak, you had to be bitten by a louse; but although we were well versed in entomology, neither of us had seen this particularly repulsive predator at close quarters. This one, fat and sluggish, was taken off with a pair of tweezers and put under a glass to await Mama's identification.

'Of course it's a louse!' was Mama's alarmed verdict.

'It hasn't bitten me,' I assured her, but she continued to worry. The incubating period for the disease was ten days and she marked her diary accordingly. On the tenth day I had forgotten all about it, but she took my temperature and was relieved to find me fit and well, so I went to school as usual. That evening I had a very slight headache but, anxious not to alarm Mama, I did not mention it. I woke up in the night, my head was splitting and I was bathed in sweat. When Mama took my temperature she did not require a doctor to diagnose my illness and, when he came, he only confirmed her fears. There was little he could do—there were no drugs of any kind—and Mama's medicine chest contained only a negligible amount of quinine. He prescribed enemas morning and evening and no solid food whatsoever. My only hope of survival would be my constitution, already weakened by three years of famine, and Mama's devoted nursing.

Of my illness I remember little. For days I lay semiconscious as Mama and Tousia relieved each other at my side. Occasionally I felt strong hands turning me over and ministering to me as both wondered, they later told me, whether my heart would be strong enough to withstand the unabating fever. I had lost count of time, saw distorted dream shapes and when, at intervals, I did regain consciousness, I felt so weak I could not speak. Even to swallow an administered spoonful of liquid was an effort which sent me back into oblivion.

It seems I hovered between life and death for about a month when, one day, I became conscious of voices in the adjoining room. I recognised Mama's but it took me some time to understand that she was talking to the doctor. My mind kept wandering as I tried to listen and I had missed the beginning of the conversation.

'You can't take her with you,' I suddenly heard the doctor say. 'She'll die en route.' It took a few minutes more to grasp that they were talking about me.

'I can't leave her behind, either,' I heard Mama's reply.

'Be reasonable, Lioubov Nikolaevna, this state of affairs is not going to last. You know it can't. She can stay with us and I will send her to you as soon as she is better. Believe me, it's her only chance!'

I could hear him pace up and down as he delivered his verdict, while I lay there stunned by the fear of dying.

'I give you my solemn word of honour I will send her out to you,' he reiterated.

'Suppose you cannot? Suppose this régime lasts? I cannot abandon my daughter!'

The door of my room opened and both came towards me. I felt my mother's hand on my forehead but kept my eyes closed. I did not want them to know I had overheard.

The doctor reached for my pulse. 'She's sleeping peacefully now and at last the temperature has receded. She may be over the worst but by no means out of the wood. The slightest jerk may prove fatal and pierce her intestines and you talk of taking her on a long journey!'

They both tiptoed out leaving the door ajar. I now strained my ears and listened intently. Slowly I began to piece together what must have happened. We had been ordered to leave Russia in the next twenty-four hours. This was the convoy which we had expected for so long. It would comprise about thirty French nationals and was our last chance of getting out. Thereafter the French Government declined all responsibility for our safety. That much was clear to me.

'Mama cannot leave me!' I thought, absolutely terrified.

Mama continued explaining to the doctor why we were being pushed out in such a hurry.

'I am told the French Fleet in the Black Sea is threatening to bombard Odessa unless all French hostages and their families are released by a certain time. It seems they are exchanging each one of us for a hundred bolsheviks!'

'What about your husband and your brother-in-law? Have you had any news?'

'Not yet. I did ask for an assurance that they would be on the train, but there has only been stony silence. You know what they are like. And you ask me to leave my daughter behind when I am not even sure of my husband's fate!'

'I know, I know.' The doctor's voice was reassuring as he tried to help Mama reach a decision. 'Why not put it to the child? She will perhaps know whether she wants to stay behind for a few weeks or go with you. She is still very weak but she is about to regain full consciousness,' he suggested.

A tremor of apprehension went through me and inwardly I panicked. I was scared to remain without Mama and Tousia, but would I die if I went with them?

Again they entered my room and as Mama bent over to kiss me, I opened my eyes.

'How are you feeling, darling?'

'Much better. I think I am all right,' I answered as she sat down beside me and gently took my hand.

'Do you think you can understand if I tell you something?'

I nodded. She then explained the situation exactly as I had understood it, but I did not let on.

'You are still very weak, darling,' she continued. 'The doctor thinks it would be more prudent if you stayed with him for a few weeks and joined us when you are stronger.'

'Don't leave me behind, Mama, don't leave me! I want to go with you. Please, please, Mama!' I begged.

She might forget all about me, I might never see her again, such terrible things could happen. 'Please God,' I prayed, 'if I am to die, let it be in Mama's arms.'

Surprised by my sudden outburst, Mama tried to comfort me. 'Of course, darling, you can come. I only asked because I did not know what you would prefer.'

But by now I was very sorry for myself. I sobbed and sobbed. I did not want to die and the doctor had sounded so emphatic.

The news that we were leaving spread like wildfire and a procession of well-wishers came round in no time. Olga Vasilievna, who was with Lera, I had not seen since Tania's death. How she had changed! She was no longer even pretty. Would Mama also lose her looks if I were to die? Uncle Kostia, released from prison a fortnight before, came post haste. As usual he comforted Mama.

'She'll be all right,' he said, looking in my direction. 'She has improved already.'

How I welcomed his words, but could I believe them after what the doctor had said?

Everyone was talking in small groups and offering advice. Lera and I whispered in the corner on my bed.

Mama and Tousia went to the attic to retrieve the hidden jewelry, only to discover that one of the caches, where the diamond necklace had been, was now empty!

'The actor must have found it,' Mama exclaimed.

But time was short. Faithful Nadejda, Kirianovna's daughter and for many years Mama's faithful seamstress, was already busy concealing the remaining jewelry by sewing it into clothes and linings. Someone suggested I should be padded with some of it. A sick child was less likely to be searched. The idea was so exciting that, for a moment, it drove away the fear of death.

As Nadejda picked up Mama's beautiful solitaire diamond ear-rings, Mama had second thoughts.

'No Nadejda. These had better stay with you until I return.'

Nadejda smiled and slipped the ear-rings quite casually into her apron pocket and nothing more was said.

The Red Rose factory, as it is now called, looks much the same today as it did at the turn of the century, except that a statue of Lenin has replaced the ornamental garden inside the main gates

The author on a recent visit to Moscow

'Douchka,' Lera whispered, 'how I wish I was coming with you. You gone and no Tania, I shall be quite alone.'

In the excitement of the last few hours I had forgotten Tania. Suddenly, it all came back. Our friendship so abruptly ended, the joys and fears we had experienced and now, perhaps, my journey into the unknown.

'Lera, I am going to die also, I know I am. I overheard the doctor tell Mama.'

At last I had shared by secret and it made me feel better.

'No, no,' Lera protested. 'You are already so much better. God will not allow it!' and she began to cry.

Now it was my turn to console her.

'Lera,' I said, 'I make a solemn vow. If I survive, I shall come back. We will see each other again.'

Next day, wrapped in mother's best sable coat—the one Emilia had saved—with jewelry sewn into its lining, thick woollen socks on my feet, covered with fur blankets, my mattress was put on a door which would serve as a stretcher. Philipoch, with tears streaming, kissed my hand and cried 'S'Bogom' (with God) and in his eyes there was untold misery. He was to survive our departure by only a few months, and I have always believed it is possible to die from a broken heart.

Outside the house a small crowd of well-wishers had gathered as Uncle Kostia and Alexis carried me out and through thick snow all the way to the Nikolaevsky Station. Strange sights were so familiar to the inhabitants of Moscow that no-one gave our procession a second glance. It was quite dark by the time we reached the station, which was crowded with people standing, sitting, sleeping and waiting with their assortment of bundles and suitcases while guards checked travel and identity documents. The French contingent was clustered together in a tight group. They cleared a space for my mattress, and all around me I could hear them swapping impressions and experiences, excited at the idea of leaving.

There was no train in sight. Several hours went by before a rumour spread that there would not be one that night. It was very cold as we settled down to spend the night on the platform. The station was transformed into one large bivouac. Snug and warm, I considered myself highly privileged. Mother and Tousia wrapped themselves in blankets and lay down alongside me with their heads propped up on suitcases, and Uncle Kostia and Alexis stood guard and watched over us. And so we spent the night. Morning, when it came, was grey and cold, and there was still no train. The patient crowd waited silently. This fatalistic acceptance held a curious, almost magnetic power and even communicated itself to the French, who were not used to such impassivity. The day dragged on. No-one dared to leave in case they missed the convoy, and no information was available. At 5pm it started to snow heavily again, and in the ensuing stillness we heard a distant low rumbling, almost like thunder. It grew louder and louder as it travelled along the platform. The bush telegraph was at work and, from afar, the information was being relayed that somewhere along the line a train had been sighted. At least another hour passed before a puff of steam like a small white cloud appeared on the horizon. The whole station, like some gigantic ant-heap, came alive and rushed forward to meet it. Only the French group remained where it was. Slowly and majestically, puffing and snorting, the huge engine and train entered the station. Men, women and children shoved and butted each other in a mad scramble to occupy every available nook, climbing on and into it through every opening, before it came to a standstill. The buffers and the roofs of the carriages were black with people, and the whole resembled an enormous bunch of black grapes. Although by now entirely submerged, the crowd still pressed forward.

'What chance have we?' I heard a Frenchwoman ask in despair. But unexpectedly, among all the confusion, a locomotive appeared from a siding, bringing two cattle-trucks and guards with fixed bayonets in its wake, to protect these trucks from being stormed. Frenchmen were to travel in one, Frenchwomen and children in the other. I was the first to be lifted in. Uncle Kostia tied thick ropes to a large beam running the length of the wagon and then passed these under my mattress, forming a sort of hammock to lessen the jerks. The chimney of a small stove went out through the roof not far from me. Windows, or rather slits the size of ventilators, covered with a narrow mesh grille, would provide the only light and air once the cattle-truck's doors were closed, and I could sniff a strong smell of creosite all around me, thanks to which the lice and bugs were, for once, absent. A thick carpet of clean straw covered the wooden floor.

'This is how cattle used to travel,' Mama cheerfully explained.

First Alexis, then Uncle Kostia bent over me and kissed me. Uncle Kostia looked boyish and very pale. He had always been very close to us. As he now turned towards Mama, was he thinking of their past journeys when he had chaperoned her on some gay jaunt? The hard ache of parting was clearly visible on both their faces as I watched them in each other's arms. Did they perceive that the flood would engulf everything they had ever known? Did they have a premonition that this was a final separation? They certainly appeared more affected than I had ever seen them, yet they had never been in the habit of displaying their emotions. The poignant scene affected me, but I too was by now accustomed to the acceptance of inevitable sorrows and Mama had taught me to put on a brave front.

The rest of the women scrambled in, helped by the men throwing their belongings after them. The guards unceremoniously pushed Alexis and Uncle Kostia out, closed and bolted the iron doors and so obliterated our last sight of Moscow.

I surveyed the scene below me which was like a gipsy encampment. The stove, which had been lit, smoked at first, then burned brightly and threw off so much heat that some of my blankets had to come off. Although we were locked up, there was already a great feeling of relief engendered by the thought that soon we would be leaving this land of terror for safer shores. The sadness of the last goodbyes was still with us but slowly a degree of happiness returned. There was no shortage of food, we had all prepared for this exodus for days. . . .

Amid a gaiety which had been absent for so long, people were able to exchange ideas for the first time in years. Completely cut off from the Western world, no-one knew for certain what was happening where. The big worry was the prisoners. Where and when would the bolsheviks produce them? As everyone reassured each other, they remembered that the French ultimatum had been precise; it had stated that all French nationals were to be exchanged. Some of us hoped that perhaps the prisoners had been sent to the Finnish frontier, ahead of our convoy.

Had I not been aware how critically ill I was, I am sure I would have guessed because of the pity in everybody's eyes! Later I was told that not one of them had expected me to survive.

Only Mama and I were of a different opinion. I clung to life and had no intention of dying and she clung to hope and, concentrating all her love on me, was determined to pull me through. Between us, with God's help, we accomplished the impossible.

CHAPTER ELEVEN

Our train, due to leave at 8pm, still stood with all of us solidly padlocked in the now empty station at past midnight. Nevertheless we were grateful not to spend a second night on the platform. Cosy in my hammock, I dozed off to be awakened by the noise of the wagon doors as they were pulled open. Two Red Guards jumped in. Was this a final search? The men looked around, opened suitcases and peered into handbags, but it was only a half-hearted effort. I looked down from my 'hammock'. I had nothing to fear, as until now I had been treated with the utmost consideration. So when the two men approached my bunk, I was quite prepared to answer the usual questions as to whether or not I was hiding something.

Suddenly two pairs of grubby hands were pulling the blankets and furs off my emaciated body. Comatose I may have been, and desperately weak, but the dread of being touched and perhaps rolled over was uppermost in my mind. The doctor had recommended the utmost care, the slightest bump could prove fatal. How dare they touch me? Fear invaded me with such a power of desperation that I screamed at the top of my voice, trying to bite the men at the same time.

'Leave me alone, how dare you, can't you see I am dying?' I yelled, hate rising and bitter tears flowing.

The soldiers were taken aback. They must have thought I was too weak to protest and too ill to care. They had not expected a little virago ready to bite and scratch. Now, making signs to each other, they departed meekly while I continued to pursue them with hysterical invective. My rage had turned to frenzy and I could not stop. The outburst left me so exhausted that it provoked general concern, and almost at once I fell into a deep sleep.

When I came to we were on the move. The wagon fell hot and stuffy and my pillow was soaking wet. Around me all was quiet but my stirring woke Mama who lay immediately below me on the straw-covered floor. She gave me a spoonful of medicine which sent me into oblivion again.

With a violent jostle the train came to a sudden stop. Mama was up in a flash, solicitous and tender.

'Are you all right, darling, are you in pain?'

'I think my intestines have burst,' I announced pompously.

With the natural fear of a child who thought she was going to die, I craved Mama's constant reassurance, which I invariably received. I think without it and without Tousia's and her love, I would have given up the fight.

And so the slow journey north continued, the convoy barely dragging itself. From time to time the doors were unbolted from outside and the occupants rushed out to relieve themselves, to fetch boiling water if we were in a station, or to help to saw wood to fuel the engine. No-one was allowed towards the rear where a sealed wagon had, at some time, been attached. Did it contain our loved ones? All hoped so.

On the third night, when we stopped again, I could see through one of the slits that we were in the middle of a snow-covered emptiness and complete silence surrounded us. In that stillness, suddenly, men's voices could be heard singing: '*Meunier, tu dors, ton moulin va trop vite, Meunier, tu dors, ton moulin va trop fort.*' The French song came over crystal clear and it unmistakeably came from the rear of the train. We all listened with bated breath. The singing grew louder.

'Hurray,' the occupants of both wagons shouted together, as if by pre-arrangement. Then a voice cried out: '*Si tous les hôtages sont ici, chantez encore.*' '*Meunier, tu dors*' came over louder than ever. We kissed and hugged each other joyfully. Next time Tousia was let out, she came back with a scrap of paper slipped to her by one of the guards. It was in Papa's writing and it finally reassured us.

The nearer to the Finnish frontier we approached, the more our spirits rose. On the morning of the seventh day the sound of cheering woke me up. The doors of the cattle-truck burst open and in jumped Papa and Uncle Paul. At last, the French hostages were reunited with their families.

Four officers of the French Mission in uniform and wearing their decorations, unhooked my makeshift hammock and carefully transferred me to a stretcher provided by the Finns. Thus

The jeweller, at first, claimed that Mama could not have afforded such a necklace. 'Few people could,' he said. Mama was furious. The French Foreign Office had a list of all the property we had lost in Russia. They sent a representative who testified in Mama's favour. Furthermore, the necklace had been bought by my father in Nice, in 1907, only round the corner from where it had come back to roost. The police were able to inspect the firm's books and found a description and a record of its sale to Papa. They also traced it back to a vice-consul in Finland, brother of the actor Mama had so distrusted! He, of course, claimed it was a family heirloom. Although it was established that the necklace was Mama's, it had passed legitimately through too many hands. A large sum would have to be paid in compensation if we were to retrieve it and my parents were by now really poor.

The jeweller, furious no doubt that for so many months he had been prevented from selling it, told the judge: 'Your Honour, we would all be out of business if all Russian refugees were to claim jewellery which once belonged to them.'

In 1929 I went to work in Paris, and sometimes returned to Nice for a weekend.

I was there with mother one day when the bell of the villa rang, and I made a move to go to the door.

'Where are you going?' Mama asked.

'To open the door.'

'What for?'

The bell rang again.

'Someone is at the door, Mother,' I said. 'Can't you hear the bell?'

'Have you invited a guest?' she asked, instead of answering me.

'No.'

'Then why open? We never do unless we are expecting someone.'

'But Mother,' I said indignantly, 'how do you know it's not important?'

She looked at me, then shook her head.

'Do as you please,' she said. 'It's immaterial.'

I knew this attitude of hers well by now. Both my parents had given up the fight and lived with their memories, and often I found them discussing a world which no longer existed. 'We've seen and done and experienced it all, even prison,' they used to say.

I opened the door to a nondescript stranger who asked to see Mother.

'I am her daughter; perhaps you could tell me what it is about?'

'I am sure, mademoiselle, your mother would wish to see me. I have brought her a message from someone she knew in Moscow.'

I asked him in and Mama received him, little suspecting what was to come. The man explained he had worked at an embassy in Moscow. 'I believe, madame, you had a faithful servant called Natalia Kirianovna?'

'Yes, she was my cook,' Mama replied, wondering what the man was driving at.

'It so happens that her granddaughter, Alexandra Matvevna, came to work at the embassy as a secretary and we became friends,' he went on.

No-one had ever called Shourka by her full name, and it took Mama some time to gather who Alexandra Matvevna was.

'The day I left Russia she asked me to give you this,' the stranger said, and putting his hand in his pocket he handed Mama a tiny parcel. Mama unwrapped it to find her diamond ear-rings. Before she had time to recover from her surprise, the stranger bowed and made a move towards the door.

'Monsieur, who are you? I must be able to thank you,' she stammered.

'Madame, the biggest service you can render me is not to try and find out my identity, nor to mention this to anyone for a good many years,' he answered, and was gone.

Mama, completely stunned, at first could hardly speak. Then we wondered who the mysterious stranger could have been?

'Do you think he was Russian?' Papa asked.

'It's impossible to tell,' she answered. 'Certainly he had no accent.'

'When I opened the door, he spoke in French and I thought he was a Frenchman,' I said.

For days we puzzled over it. Shourka had been courted by a prominent communist. Did she marry him? Had she thus become a trusted member of the party and been given a job at an embassy? That Kirianovna was devoted to us as well as Nadejda, none of us had ever doubted, but Shourka, the granddaughter, was the new generation and, as such, her loyalty was often in question. The more we tried to disentangle the whole story, the more incredible it became. The man who had brought the diamonds must have suspected their value. He need not have delivered them—no-one would have been any the wiser!

The enigma remained unsolved, but one thing was certain; those diamonds were worth a small fortune, being ten carats each and blue-white! Their subsequent sale enabled my parents to live reasonably again, and such surely unique integrity and honesty did much to restore their faith in human nature.

Years went by. As long as my parents were alive, there could be no question of my revisiting Russia. 'Why turn the dagger in their hearts?' I thought. 'They have suffered enough.' But, left alone, the atavistic craving to return to my mother's country and see conditions there for myself, and maybe to find Uncle Kostia's family, steadily grew. That is how, in the summer of 1970 and with three friends (I dreaded going alone), I undertook my first and shattering journey.

Part Two

A Tourist in Russia

CHAPTER TWELVE

Three and a half hours' flying-time from London, the half-empty Illyushin touched down at Moscow Airport. After fifty years away I was in Russia again, this time as a tourist.

Our passports were examined by officials who were little more than boys, who made very heavy weather of the fact that our visas ran from 9 July 1970 and we were arriving on the eighth. I explained that the London office of Intourist had advised us to travel on the eighth because there was no suitable plane on the ninth, but the decision to let us in was considerably delayed by their endless head-scratching, buck-passing and consultations. Customs clearance went better, and soon the four of us were travelling in two chauffeur-driven taxis and an Intourist guide in each towards Moscow.

Sheremetevo Airport is about twenty-five kilometres from Moscow and not far from Himki, where my family once had an estate. We were travelling the Leningrad road, the former St. Petersburg Chaussée which we had so often used on our way out to Himki, but nothing remained of the small, wooden villages or the golden cupolas of its churches. There was nothing here that I could recognise, except a few birch trees here and there to remind me it was Russia, and soon even these were replaced by the ugly buildings of Moscow sprawling out over what had once been open country.

The advertisement hoardings of the West were replaced here by red posters and political slogans flashing monotonously past, all praising the communist régime. For some reason the effect of this propaganda was very grim and depressing. So was the Metropole Hotel in Red Square when we finally ascended its dirty steps. The hall looked like a railway station; there were no carpets and the only furniture was a bench or two; only a forlorn chandelier and a painted ceiling remained to testify to the hotel's former grandeur. Our passports were taken from us and rooms allocated, and we had a long session in the Intourist office exchanging the vouchers we had bought in London for coupons entitling us to lunches, breakfasts, dinners, excursions, theatre tickets and everything else for which we had contracted in London. The paperwork involved in issuing the coupons and taking particulars of our names, our date of arrival and so on seemed very laborious, but the allocation of coupons was extremely generous. We could not use all of them, and at the end of our stay we were allowed to use them to pay for caviar, vodka and souvenirs with the remainder.

When all the formalities were over we were allowed to go to our rooms, which were on the top floor. They were clean enough, in fact they smelt strongly of carbolic, but they were furnished only with the bare essentials. The sheets just covered the mattresses, with no tuck-in, and everything was of the poorest and cheapest quality. But there was a private bathroom, and at least everything seemed to work!

As soon as we had unpacked and tidied up we went down to the restaurant, found a table and sat down. The orchestra was blaring and waiters were rushing around but nobody took any notice of us. Martine and I were not particularly hungry; we decided to have a look at the town before we went to bed, so we left our companions in the restaurant and went out into Red Square.

It was nearly midnight. The Kremlin with its crimson walls and blue and gold cupolas had not changed, except that the cross on the top had been replaced by a red star. It was beautifully illuminated, romanticised by the lights, and for a moment I could imagine that I was back in the Russia of my childhood; but the crowds of people who surrounded us, badly dressed, unsmiling and preoccupied, brought me back to reality. We walked past *Gum* and I recognised my father's offices, which seemed little changed, and we pressed on through the crowds in the direction of the house where I was born, using the Bolshoi Theatre as a landmark.

I knew from reading modern guide-books that the old names had been replaced by unfamiliar modern ones, as surely as Lenin had replaced all that Russia had ever worshipped. The wide streets seemed never-ending, and the distances far greater than I remembered. On our right the *Manège* still stood, but further on the Cathedral of our Saviour, once the most richly decorated church in Moscow, had been demolished to make way for the Palace of Congresses. For some reason the foundations would not hold, so it had been turned into a large swimming-pool instead. Later I was told that many Russians, as superstitious as ever, cross themselves furtively as they pass and attribute the drownings which sometimes occur there to God's displeasure. I was saddened by the disappearance of this truly Russian monument, in all its Oriental splendour. Later I discovered some of the frescoes and bas reliefs which had once adorned it leaning against a wall in the Donskoy Cemetery, exposed to the weather and slowly deteriorating.

By now we had walked quite a distance, and the fatigue of a day's travelling was beginning to overtake us. We arrived at the junction of two streets which have now been renamed, but which I knew as the Ostogenka and the Pritchistinka. The Pritchistinka, now called Kropotkin Street, used to consist of private houses; my school had been there too, and sure enough after walking a few hundred yards we came upon the building standing in its courtyard. It had been converted into a library, and there was nothing to indicate that it had once been a fashionable school for young ladies. A portrait of Lenin hung above the entrance.

On crisp winter mornings Matvei used to boast that he could drive me from our house to school in three minutes flat; the pair of black horses knew the way, and the sleigh simply flew. But now it was late, and I was tired, and I decided not to continue looking for my old home. 'Let's call it a day,' I said to my companion.

Thinking that there might be a shorter way back, I approached a woman who had just come out of the Metro. 'How far are we from the Metropole Hotel?' I asked.

She obviously took me for a Russian. 'It's quite a distance. Too far to walk. Take the underground,' she said.

She was badly dressed and looked tired, obviously a poor woman in a miserable country, returning from a hard day's work. We had no Russian money and it had been impressed upon us that it was dangerous and illegal to change foreign currency on the street. I started to explain all this, but she interrupted me. 'I'll give you two five-kopek coins; that's all you need,' and she dived into her pocket to help a couple of total strangers as if it was the most natural thing in the world.

'No, no,' I protested. We thanked her and walked in the direction she had indicated. The street was dark and eerie, but a few minutes later a ghost-like figure appeared from nowhere and I went up to her to check that we were going in the right direction. 'Are you foreigners?' she asked, before I had time to open my mouth, and when I nodded she gave me a startled, frightened glance, mumbled something unintelligible and disappeared into the night. Somewhat unnerved, we became even more eager to return to the comparative security of our hotel. We quickened our pace and soon reached the *Manège*, where we asked a militia man if he could get us a taxi. He was most amiable, and eager to talk to a foreigner who could speak his own language, if only to temper the boredom of his spell on duty. He blew his whistle and a taxi pulled up.

'Take these tourists to the Metropole Hotel,' he ordered, with no please or thankyou. Men in authority speak in a very snappy, curt and monosyllabic manner to their fellow Russians, though to us they were invariably very polite. I soon discovered that it often paid off not to speak Russian; if I did I was brushed aside as one of their compatriots. Instead I developed a very effective technique, which consisted of establishing that I was a foreigner by speaking English or French very loudly, before going over to Russian.

The driver took us in complete silence to the Metropole Hotel. He neither asked for nor received payment. Back in our dingy room we went to bed. The first day in Russia was over without any great emotional disturbances.

Next morning I waited for the *bureau de change* to open. I needed Russian coins to telephone Mitia, who was the son of our doctor and my only link with the past. There are no telephone directories in Russia, and it was by a lucky chance that I knew his number. The night before the hotel porter had offered to put me through to him, but I was acutely aware of the risks involved, and I didn't know that local calls from hotels in the Soviet Union are free. There were no foreign papers on sale at the kiosk, apart from *L'Humanité*, but they had some small badges of Lenin. Martine had professed a great attachment to him, even threatening to visit his mausoleum, so for a joke

I decided to buy her one of these badges. 'Is this ten kopeks?' I asked the attendant.

She glared at me without answering, so I repeated the question. 'Yes,' she shouted angrily, 'it is ten kopeks, but it isn't "this", it's Lenin!'

I dialled Mitia's number from a public call-box. He must have been waiting, for he answered at once. Our conversation was brief; I gave him the number of my room at the hotel, and he was there within twenty minutes. He was a slight, ederly man; we fell into each other's arms, choked with emotion. As soon as we had recovered our composure, he whispered, 'Let's go to my place—there we can talk.'

After the dinginess of the hotel, the delapidation of the buildings, and the drabness, poverty and lack of paint which the illuminations had concealed and the morning had revealed, the metro was palatial, and not only by comparison. It was so striking that I wondered if the régime had built it as a sort of compensation for all the beauty it had destroyed. In the crowded train my childhood companion was the only one wearing a collar and tie. He had the fine, sensitive face of an artist, and a slightly bitter expression. His whole appearance was very neat; his clothes were old but carefully brushed and pressed, and his manner was quiet and unobtrusive. I remarked upon his tie.

'I put it on especially for you,' he replied. Later I found out that it was the only one he possessed.

While the train rattled along at high speed, Mitia explained where we were going, told me how many stations we would pass before we came to our destination, and talked enthusiastically about his new flat. It had all the amenities one could wish for, and his praise was extravagant. From the station we walked for ten minutes past ugly tenements until we came to a building no better and no worse than the rest. On the first landing Mitia opened one of the doors and ushered me into his paradise. There was a tiny entrance lobby, *one* medium-sized room, a small kitchen and a bathroom. A large table in the middle of the room was covered with a plastic tablecloth; above it a naked bulb hung from the ceiling. There were half-a-dozen chairs and two divan beds; and in the corner, incongruously, a large Victorian mahogany wardrobe. There was a single French window with a small balcony, and two window boxes full of scarlet beans. Unexpectedly, the walls were almost covered by paintings—landscapes, nudes, flowers. Mitia's wife, seeing my surprise, explained that painting was Mitia's hobby. It had to remain a hobby because he was not a registered artist, and had therefore no right to sell his paintings! I was struck by the poverty of their home and its contents—there was nothing of any value. And yet they both spoke with such gusto and joy of how much easier life had become, and of their wonderful new flat. They asked about relatives and friends, and we took a count of who was dead and who had survived. After so many years words did not come easily.

'What has happened to Hanochka?' I asked.

'She died last year. She was eighty-six and going blind.'

'And her son, Leo?' (The little boy who had grown up in our house.)

'I don't know. She lived alone for the last ten years and we never spoke about him.'

'Yet you saw her often?' (How strange his answers were!)

'Oh yes. As often as I could. She was truly a remarkable woman.' At this Mitia's wife nodded in agreement.

'What about Lera?'

He shook his head and from his expression I knew it was useless to question him further. He promptly changed the subject.

I had to tread very carefully, as anything I said was liable to be misconstrued. We were on totally different wavelengths, and communication was very difficult. I told him I wanted to revisit some of the places I had known. Would he be prepared to be my guide? I explained that Moscow had become so immense that I felt quite lost.

'Would you like me to arrange a reunion with some of those you once knew?' he asked suddenly. 'That is, if they consent to come,' a remark which, at the time, I failed to understand.

We made our plans for the next day and went back to the hotel on the underground, this time getting out at every station so that I could examine and admire everything. We parted at the hotel entrance and I rejoined my three companions in the restaurant.

The orchestra was playing louder than ever. We had to shout into each other's ears. Russians, who looked to me like Party members, danced every dance—old-fashioned tangos and fox-trots—and were obviously enjoying themselves. They all gaped when occasionally a foreign couple danced in a more modern way. Someone waved to us, and we recognised two Greek men we had met the previous night in the Intourist office. One of them came over and asked us if we would like to join them for coffee in the café where one paid in foreign currency.

Meanwhile we waited, but no-one came to take our order. The restaurant was like an old-fashioned Lyons' Corner House. There were white damask tablecloths and napkins, and the waiters looked quite presentable. Finally an old man brought us the menu and some bread. There were a lot of items to choose from, but only a few were priced. We found out later that the unpriced items were hardly ever available. They were listed, I daresay, just to impress foreigners.

Half-an-hour later the waiter took our order. We started with caviar at eight shillings (40p) per portion; Mary and Agnes opted for cold fish and salad, but Martine and I ordered Wiener schnitzel as a main course. We knew it would be a long-drawn-out disaster, having learnt from the experience of Mary and Agnes the night before, but we were born optimists, we had nothing better to do, and so we sat and waited. One hour passed. I managed to catch the waiter's eye, and twenty minutes later the caviar, cold fish and salad arrived. We tucked in, expecting the rest to follow; we polished off all the bread on the table, but still there was no sign of the Wiener schnitzel. I beckoned to the waiter, who promised emphatically that he would bring it right away. After more waiting it finally arrived three hours after we had entered the restaurant. I cut a piece and put it in my mouth and got the shock of my life; the outside was hot, but the inside was frozen solid. It must have been taken out of the freezer in such a hurry that it had not thawed out. Martine and I dissolved in fits of uncontrollable laughter, and when we explained the cause of our mirth Agnes, in her most imperturbable manner, said: 'You should send it back.'

'What!' I replied. 'And wait another two hours?'

The waiter, who was a pleasant old boy, realised what was wrong and was very contrite. He ran off to the kitchens, reappearing almost at once with all kinds of salads and cold dishes which we had not ordered, did not want, and for which he did not attempt to charge us.

Afterwards we joined the Greeks for coffee. They had come over on business, after endless correspondence, in the hope that they might be able to bring a deal to a successful conclusion. But nothing had been as they had expected and, thoroughly disheartened, they were leaving for Athens the next day. They gave us a colourful and amusing account of their frustration, but I never imagined that our encounter would also be profitable. Early next morning Martine knocked at my door. The Greeks wanted to know if we would like roubles worth seventy-five dollars, and at the black-market rate of exchange, six times the official rate! I jumped at the chance, and thereafter we had no financial troubles.

Mitia came at the appointed time, but when I told him that my first call was at a foreign embassy, his face clouded over. I reassured him and told him that he could wait around the corner. I gave his some roubles (money was obviously in short supply) saying that if he was to be guide he had better be banker too.

Transport, apparently, was going to be a problem. It was one thing to be a tourist, treated like some kind of VIP, and quite another to be an ordinary Russian citizen. From the hotel to the embassy we hired a taxi, but the driver refused to wait for us there. Mitia wanted to take us to Vorobieve Gori for a panoramic view of the city but wasn't sure which tram would take us there. He asked a passer-by. Mitia was thirteen at the time of the Russian revolution, and he had not been able to drop the slight accent, a sort of French r, that some educated Russians used to have. His voice still sounds refined, and evidently the stranger spotted this at once. 'Can't you read?' he growled aggressively, pointing to a sign. Mitia did not reply, but I was fast getting the impression that there was little civility left, that the language had become more coarse, and that refinement of any kind was regarded as bourgeois prejudice.

The view from the hills was lovely, but I was disappointed by the disappearance of the onion-shaped cupolas of the four hundred churches which used to adorn the town and which made it look so typically Russian. The Kremlin was still there but the modern building of the Palace of Congresses seemed strangely out of place. As for Mitia, he was most impressed by the television tower, clearly visible in the bright summer light.

'Look at it!' he kept repeating. 'You must visit it. It's higher than the Eiffel Tower!'

'I'm not very interested in technical achievements,' I said. 'I'd rather see my old home.'

So we walked alongside the Moskva river and took a river tram to Hamovniki, the nearest stop to a short-cut which used to lead directly to our house. I recognised it all; nothing much had changed, except that it looked as if nobody cared. The main entrance-gates, boarded up on my father's orders to keep out stray bullets, remained exactly as they had been when I last saw them, and blocked the view into the courtyard. Mitia stood at some distance. He did not want to get involved. Nor did my friends, to whom it meant nothing. But I was determined to see my old home, and I went up to the gates and succeeded in hoisting myself up sufficiently to catch a glimpse of the top of the roof. A rude, angry female voice shouted: 'Get off there, it is forbidden to look!'

'It is not forbidden. I was born there sixty years ago and I want to look.' There was a gasp and a woman of about forty appeared. She eyed me from top to toe and then, with a reverence in her voice which surprised me, said 'You must be one of them!'

As if by magic, the side gate was opened and I found myself in the janitor's lodge. Friendly faces surrounded me, all wanting to know why and from where I had come. I beckoned my friends to join me. More workers of both sexes were gathering around us, all apparently anxious to look at me, and all apparently benevolent in intention. When I asked to see the house, they discussed which official to contact to get permission, and one of the women went off while we sat and waited. I answered a great many questions; I could not have dreamt of such a reception, and I was very flattered.

After about fifteen minutes the first woman came back with another carrying a large bunch of keys. 'You want to see the house?' she said, beaming at me and shaking hands. 'I'll show it to you. There is still a wonderful fireplace you will recognise.'

The outside of the house was exactly as I remembered it, except for the peeling paint. In front of my mother's windows, where there had once been a fountain surrounded by flowers, there was now the inevitable statue of Lenin wearing a cloth cap and haranguing some political meeting. Martine was about to take a photograph, but the woman stopped her, saying 'I might get into trouble.'

We mounted the familiar steps, the woman fiddled for a moment with the keys and threw the door open. Instead of the hall —my memory was suddenly very vivid—there was nothing. The house was just a shell, stripped down to its very foundations and boarded up with planks of wood, painted green. It was like a blacked-out chicken run. Our guide pushed aside a plywood partition and pointed proudly to a green marble fireplace in a corner.

'There it is!' she whispered conspiratorially.

In my mind's eye I could suddenly see our old butler Philipoch sitting in his high chair close to that fireplace, listening for the sound of the carriage or the car coming down the street. Opening the door to welcome the return of my parents was a duty he performed at any time of day or night.

I turned to the woman. 'Is there nothing else?' I was hardly able to speak.

She shook her head. She saw that I was upset. 'It was like that when I came,' she said apologetically.

I walked out of my old home completely stunned, and my companions followed me silently. At the janitor's lodge the crowd still waited, and an old woman came up to me, crossed herself and murmured 'I've known all your family.'

'So much the better, grandma,' I replied, carrying my head high and hoping I looked dignified. I tried not to show my emotion, but I think I must have failed, for one of the women grabbed my hand and kissed it, much to my surprise. 'Thank you for coming,' she said. 'We have done what we could—all we could.' I wondered what she meant and I *still* wonder. Mitia was furious, and went very red in the face.

'You didn't know you were born in a hovel, did you?' he hissed. 'Whatever possessed you to want to see the place again?'

I did not reply. The woman had said that in two years' time it was scheduled for demolition. I wished that it had been pulled down earlier.

CHAPTER THIRTEEN

Mitia had promised to take me to Himki, where we once had an estate. It was then country, but it is now a suburb about twenty-five kilometres from Moscow. Together, perhaps, we might be able to find the house. Mitia suggested we should take the metro out to the Fluvial station, which—as far as I could judge—was built on land that was once attached to my uncle's summer residence; we could start looking from there.

The Fluvial station, like most Russian public buildings, turned out to be very imposing. It was large and attractive, and it stood on the bank of the Moskva at the junction of several important inland waterways; boats started here for the Volga and for many other canals, of which Russia has a great many.

The station was quite grandiose, and boasted a fair selection of amenities, including a restaurant with terraces leading down to the river. The difference between the luxury of public buildings in Russia and the drabness and poverty of ordinary people's homes is quite striking, but it is perhaps something that has its origins before the revolution; in the Russia of my childhood people had flocked to the churches for the sake of the ceremony, pomp and beauty. Perhaps it is simply that the 'opium of the people' has been replaced by the Palace of Congresses and the Fluvial station and their like.

I had wanted to start out from the station at Himki—if it was still there—and walk to the house three miles away. So at the Fluvial we took a bus which shook our guts out carreering across ploughed ground where bulldozers were levelling the soil for more building. For twenty minutes we travelled through a flattened countryside where nothing remained of the tiny villages and the landscapes I had known. We stopped at a little yellow station that, in the middle of this desolation, was exactly as it had been fifty years before. Time here had waited for me. But the single-track line had grown to three, and there was an overhead bridge where previously you simply crossed the line and scrambled up the steep bank on the other side. It used to be covered in golden cowslips in the spring, which reminded my governess, Miss Baines, of her home in England. In summer wild strawberries could be found there in profusion. From here I was quite sure of the direction to take.

But this was no longer open country, and there was no sign of a private road; it had become a garden suburb of rather ugly houses. We plodded on, hoping to find a familiar landmark such as the lake; finally Mitia stopped an old woman.

'Is there an old *dacha* in the direction we are going?'

'Yes, you are on the right track, you'll find it further on.'

Soon we came to a large expanse of water. Tractors were at work excavating, and a seven-storey building was being erected where the water had already been filled in. It was impossible to be sure whether it was the lake, or whether they really were filling it in, but certainly on the opposite bank the ground rose as I had remembered it. If this was the place, the house should be a little further on. We crossed waste ground, making our way through weeds, broken-down fences and litter until suddenly we were confronted by a high, wooden fence so close to a house that I could only see its roof. I tried to find a hole to peep through, but there was none. It was impossible to see in, and the place was ominously silent. It looked like some kind of institution; the only gate was padlocked, and I found myself wondering whether it might be one of those 'mental homes' where people who express their thoughts too freely are locked up. It was difficult to be sure whether it was our old *dacha* or not, and the surrounding country-side had been transformed. We searched in vain for clues; I wondered whether the circle of pines just outside the fence marked the spot where my parents had been in the habit of entertaining people for dinner on summer evenings, but perhaps it was just wishful thinking.

We sat down in a small clearing and reminisced. Mitia told me about the terrible days after we left Russia. Uncle Kostia had died of heart failure at forty-eight, and Aunt Miloucha was arrested because of her connection with us—capitalists and foreigners. She was kept in prison for six months and questioned periodically, apparently in an attempt to find out where our family had buried jewellery and other valuables.

'How could she know?' I interrupted. Poor, simple Aunt Miloucha had never been in my parents' confidence; all she ever thought about was her children.

'They didn't believe her,' Mitia went on, 'and when they finally let her go they took away her ration card.'

I knew what that meant; many people had starved that way. I remembered Sophie, and others . . .

'Mercifully she died soon after,' Mitia added. He went on to tell me how, after his father's death, he had become the head of his family at fifteen. 'I had to look after my four younger brothers and my sister, who was only three. We lived in the cellar of our house. I was unable to continue my education because of my parentage.'

I nodded my understanding. Anyone who did not have a proletarian background had been suspect.

'I did all kinds of jobs; I swept streets, delivered buns, anything at all to earn a few coppers so that we could eat. And we survived, although I don't know how!'

All this he told me very simply, just a plain statement of facts, without any dramatisation and without bitterness. He was grateful for having come through the ordeal alive, an attitude I was to come across frequently. Now he was eager to live and enjoy life to the full. 'Don't you think life is wonderful?' he suddenly asked me, and I wondered how he could think so when I was almost reduced to tears listening to him.

Mitia suggested that we have lunch at the restaurant at the Fluvial station. A crowd was waiting outside the closed doors in front of a notice informing them that the restaurant was full. By now I had realised that a foreigner in Russia need not take no for an answer, so I pushed my way in, followed by Mitia. Mary, who was with us, somehow got left behind. Brandishing my British passport, my vouchers and foreign currency of every description, I managed to persuade the supervisor to give us a good table on the terrace, and explained I had lost a friend—also a foreign tourist—in the crowd. Soon Mary joined us, much to the annoyance of the crowd of Russians waiting at the door. We ordered caviar and other delicacies that Mitia had not tasted for years; it was a joy to be able to indulge him. He was like a little boy to whom you give a sweet.

After the waitress had brought our order, the woman supervisor returned. Like many Russians, she was curious to know where we came from and how we lived.

'Why don't you travel and find out for yourself?' I asked.

'Our government does not allow it,' she replied cheerfully.

The reunion that Mitia had organised was to take place at his brother's flat. At the Intourist office I asked for a taxi, only to be told that I should have ordered one earlier. Now it would take two hours. I had made up various gift parcels for those I was about to meet, so I was laden with carrier bags. Mary, who speaks Russian, had also been invited, so we decided to try our luck with a passing taxi which turned out to be an ambulance. But the driver of another car spotted us, slowed down and, discovering we were tourists, asked us to jump in. I switched to Russian and started a conversation.

'Where are you going?'

'Proletarskaya Street,' I replied.

'Why all the parcels?'

'We have a lot of friends.'

The driver smiled. 'Pity I'm not one of them!'

'You never know. You did promise to take us all the way there.'

'What have you got in all those parcels?'

'I told you. All sorts of presents. Is this a taxi?'

'No, no. What sort of presents?'

'Do you have a family?' I asked.

'Yes. A wife and a daughter of seventeen.'

'Well then, here's a pair of tights for your daughter.'

His face lit up and he accepted the tights gratefully.

'How come you have a car?' I asked.

'It's not mine.'

'But you told us it wasn't a taxi.'

'Of course it is. I work for Intourist, same as everybody else.'

'Then why did you pick us up?'

'Sometimes I work for myself.'

'Isn't it dangerous?'

'Of course it is. But who is to know? After all, you are foreigners.'

We drove past some women working with pickaxes on the tramlines. It looked like hard work, and it was past 7pm by now.

'Is that forced labour?' I asked.

'No, they just come from the provinces to be in a big town.

148

They don't want to work in factories, so they choose heavy work outside. They're hefty wenches. They soon get used to it. Besides, they don't work as hard as you think,' he added, laughing. 'Maybe three hours in all. The rest is spent having tea and taking it easy!'

'And you? What will you do once you've taken us to our destination?'

'I don't know.'

'Aren't you going to report back?'

He shrugged his shoulders. 'If I feel like it.'

He had difficulty finding the place. It was a new development; bulldozers were still at work and there were no signs giving the names of the streets. The heavy clay soil, wet from recent rains, was very slippery, and the car skidded a lot as we drove around looking for the address. At last we found the apartment block. By this time we had parted with a pair of tights, two bars of chocolate, chewing gum and a packet of cigarettes. We were the best of friends with our driver; not only did he refuse payment, he carried me across the mud from the taxi to the building.

When I told Mitia afterwards he reprimanded me for being recklessly extravagant, and with a stranger too. 'You gave him the equivalent of about fifteen roubles! No wonder he was pleased!'

Four men and two women were expecting us. Apart from Mitia and his wife I did not recognise anyone. I had to guess, relying on childhood memories, and I guessed wrong. There were Mitia's two brothers, Theo and Volodia, and their sister Miloucha. Theo was of medium height and heavily built, Volodia was tall and thin, with a face that told of a lifetime's suffering. Miloucha was quite good-looking, though she had made no effort to improve on nature. Her first husband had been killed in the war, and she had come with her second husband. Anatole, my own and my only cousin, the baby whose life mother had saved, had refused the invitation.

'He's still working and it is dangerous for him to associate with foreigners. Besides, he is married to the daughter of a prominent communist,' Mitia explained.

They crowded around us, asking lots of questions, obviously enjoying what was for them a very novel situation. Only Theo remained aloof, and I began to wonder why he had come. I produced two bottles of French brandy, which were opened and poured into large wine-glasses. We sat down to a quantity of *zakuski* and vodka; the window was open, the night was warm, the company congenial and the brandy conducive to confidential talk. At least I thought so. The glasses, in the best Russian tradition, were refilled as quickly as they were emptied. Theo, who sat on my left, would not touch a drop, said little and was obviously uneasy, while Volodia drank brandy as if it was wine and only complained that it was not as potent as the Russian variety.

The more they drank, the more questions they asked; they were very curious, but I could see that from time to time my answers were not what they had expected, and they would remark that 'Our propaganda machine has told us something different'. Theo kept fidgeting, saying 'For God's sake, shut up!' from time to time, or 'Don't talk so loud! Shut the window!' Occasionally he even stood up for the regime. I felt sure that he was a party member. The others had mentioned that he was the 'bigshot' of the family; he had a car, a *dacha*, two sons working on secret assignments, and he was said to have invented a number of things. . . . All this came out in bits and pieces; it was all rather mysterious, but I drew my own conclusions.

My glass was frequently refilled with vodka, and everyone began to help themselves to the food on the table. Volodia, surprised that I didn't follow suit, said 'Why aren't you eating?' and I realised that one was supposed to reach out with one's fork and grab whatever one wanted. I glanced at Mary, on the other side of the table; she, too, had got the idea now.

Plates of boiled chicken were placed in front of us. They were all eating like birds of prey, picking the bones clean. This was obviously a feast, not an everyday occasion, and they were making the best of it.

Miloucha's husband, Nikolai, was constantly being ticked off for interrupting everyone to put his questions. Now he moved next to me. 'I must hear what happened in the world at large while I was in a concentration camp,' he said.

'How did it happen? How long did they keep you?' I asked.

'Seven long years. I am a writer and a poet, and those are pretty dodgy professions in this country!' he said. He went on to say that he had heard that my family had been the most progressive and liberal employers in Russia. 'Even Lenin has praised your family in one of his books.'

'They certainly had a peculiar way of thanking us,' I remarked. 'When I was released from the concentration camp,' Nikolai went on, 'I was just a tramp. Only one pair of trousers to my name. I sat down on a bench on one of the boulevards, and that's where I met Miloucha. She had been through a lot too, and she was as lonely as I was. We got into conversation, and discovered that in 1926 we had both lived in the same street. I remembered the family. I had known them by sight, and admired their tremendous industry. They were always working! You don't know how lucky I was to find Miloucha! She is a wonderful woman. Who else would have taken me on, broken down and destitute?'

'Those seven years must have been dreadful,' I said.

He smiled sadly. 'It's too long a story and you are here for such a short time. Most of us Russians have been "inside" at some time or other. And if I were to tell you some of my experiences, there is a lot you would not believe and a lot you couldn't understand.'

How true, I thought. One cannot understand a suffering one has not been through oneself.

He listened to the BBC regularly. He knew about the dissident writers and had just heard of the Pasternak tragedy. 'Have you read Dr. Zhivago? What is it about?' When I explained he said 'Why have they banned it? It's only a description of so many of our lives!'

He begged me to bring him books when I came again. We spoke of Solzhenitsyn. He had read *One Day in the Life of Ivan Denisovich*. He did not know about *First Circle* and I promised to bring it. I was getting more and more deeply involved when Mitia interrupted us. I got the impression that they were all so eager for contact with the outside world that they each became jealous if one of the others got too much of my attention; and yet there is so little trust that they keep to themselves everything they hear. 'We never know who might betray us,' Mitia (and many others) told me.

Volodia, pouring out the last of the brandy, was getting very mellow. He put his arm around my shoulders. 'What are your plans for the future?'

I thought he meant our travel plans, but he interrupted me. 'I don't mean that, I mean your future life!'

'My dear,' I said, 'I am sixty-two and a widow. What plans *can* I have for the future? I am simply waiting for death.'

'Don't say that!' he roared, obviously very upset. 'I am sixty-five and I haven't started living yet!'

His violent outburst was so full of hope that I felt ashamed and sorry that I had mentioned death. I was beginning to feel uncomfortable, faced by realities that made even my painted nails seem frivolous and silly.

Volodia had married young—he had needed a partner to face the hardships of life in Siberia. Both he and his wife were engineers. Working in Siberia they had been more remote from the central government, and had been lucky enough to escape arrest. They had a son and a daughter. 'My son is a party member, my daughter is working in a *komsomol* at present,' he explained.

'What is that?' I asked.

He laughed. 'You are not well informed about our way of life. When there are crops to be gathered, you are drafted in to help, whatever your profession. It makes no difference whether you are highly skilled or not, or whether a single potato may thus cost five roubles. We have equality under the communist régime, and you must learn about it if you do not want to be thought ignorant.' It was impossible to tell how much of this he really meant.

They continued to question us about how we lived, how we could afford to come to the Soviet Union, what sort of rooms we had in London (a house was unimaginable), our occupations, our pastimes. Someone mentioned the churches, and how there was so little left of the Russia of my childhood.

'Do any of you believe?' I asked. They all seemed surprised at the question. After a long silence, Mitia answered. 'For fifty years it has been forbidden to speak about religion. Even Christmas trees were forbidden. If they discovered one in your home you were given a heavy sentence, maybe in a concentration camp. How do we know whether we believe when for fifty years they taught us to forget. I simply can't answer you.'

The others silently agreed. My brothers had been educated at the Imperial Lycée. Now Nicolai went on to tell me what had happened to twenty of their companions. The boys must have been about seventeen when the Tsar was so ignominiously murdered. On the first anniversary of his death they decided to hold a service for the repose of his soul. Religious persecution had started and it was not easy to find a priest, but they succeeded and the service took place one night in a wood. Someone denounced them and a few days later they were all arrested. The priest and the ringleaders were summarily shot, the others were sent to the notorious Solovki Islands, to perish there. (I later found confirmation of this story in a Russian book published in Rome.)

I had not yet distributed the presents I had brought, so Miloucha and I undid the parcels in the kitchen and discussed what would fit who. We came to the parcel I had wrapped up for the supervisor at the Fluvial restaurant who had been kind to us, containing an old jersey dress, a cake of toilet soap and a pair of stockings. When I asked Mitia to deliver this parcel sometime he asked to see the contents.

That night in our room Mary suddenly said 'I bet that dress will never reach its destination.' I, too, had had the same idea, and sure enough, before we left the Soviet Union Mitia sheepishly confessed: 'I didn't deliver your parcel. It was much too good to give to a stranger and my wife wanted the dress so badly.'

All evening Theo had been ill at ease. Now he glanced at his watch and decided that it was time to go home. I looked at Mary —maybe we should go too? Mitia immediately rushed after Theo, only to return a few seconds later looking slightly embarrassed. 'Theo says that as he has been drinking it wouldn't be wise to drive his car in to the centre of the town, so he can't give you a lift.' I knew it was a lie; he simply wanted as little as possible to do with us. Why had he bothered to come? Was it just curiosity? I never saw him again.

Now they all begged us to stay a little longer, which we suspected was so that nothing should connect us with Theo. Meanwhile they discussed how far they could safely accompany us, finally deciding that as it was late and there were few people about they would go with us to our hotel by underground.

As we approached the Metropole, two men came out supporting a third, who was hopelessly drunk and quite a disgusting sight. They tried to bundle him into a cab. In the Soviet Union the police do not arrest drunks unless they actually fall down, hence the attention this one was receiving.

'You can understand why we never go out to places like this,' Mitia said. 'Apart from the danger, there is no pleasure in seing such sights. Anyway, what friends have we left? They were all liquidated or just disappeared, and those who didn't are dead now. Occasionally we come together as a family, but even then. . . You noticed my brothers didn't want to show you their wives? It's probably safer without them.'

CHAPTER FOURTEEN

The day after the reunion was a Sunday. Mary and I decided to
go to the church of St Louis des Français, where we had both
worshipped as children. The staff at the Intourist office either
could not or would not tell us anything about it, neither the times
of the services nor whether there were any, but we were not to be
discouraged. We set off towards the Loubianka Square, passing
the statue of Djerjinsky, that great signer of death warrants, with
a shudder.

We found the church. It seemed smaller, like many of childhood's memories, but inside nothing had been changed, and I
recognised the pew where I used to sit during my catechism
lessons. Emotions and memories gripped me. I suddenly remembered the humiliation I felt there when, asked on what day
Christ was born, I could not find the answer. Now the congregation was in full song; it sounded more Orthodox than Catholic,
which surprised me until I discovered that it was now a Polish
church. It was packed, mostly with older people. We squeezed
past devoutly praying people into an empty pew; they were so
absorbed in worship that they scarcely noticed us.

A bearded young man was on his knees in the middle of
the aisle. His eyes were lifted up to heaven in an unblinking
stare, his lips moved in silent prayer and his face resembled that
of a martyr awaiting execution. The sight was deeply moving; I
have never seen anyone who seemed so nearly in ecstasy. I looked
around the church and saw that many of the worshippers, both
young and old, were in tears. Was it only in church that they
could give vent to their feelings? An oppressed nation praying
for deliverance? The ancient Jews must have prayed like that. I
had never seen such mystical fervour, not even at Lourdes. I
looked at my companions, and saw that they were as moved by
it as I was.

'Let's get out!' I said, unable to stand it any longer. These
services, I knew, went on for ever. We came out into the sunlit

courtyard, where a beggarwoman, hearing me say something in Russian, followed us. 'You must be foreigners who lived here before the revolution,' she said. 'Please, please pray for us! We have been through so much and still our sufferings continue. I am ninety-four and I have seen it all.'

I burst into tears. Most of that Sunday I longed to leave Moscow, with all its sadness, poverty and fear. I began to realise that our exile in France had been a special benediction, a blessing in disguise.

That evening Mitia telephoned. He had been out with friends on some excursion. When he told them that I, a long-lost friend, was in town, they reproached him for leaving me. 'I 'phoned you but you had already gone out. Where have you been?' he asked.

'We went to church.'

He was silent for a moment. 'Church?' He drew the word out. I had apparently mentioned the unmentionable.

The telephone rang again. Miloucha this time. She had been examining my presents and she was full of questions.

'Why the double skirt?'

'What double skirt?'

'Well, you know, a wool skirt and then another in silk inside it.'

'That is the lining.'

'Ah!' She sounded astonished. 'What for?'

'So that it doesn't lose its shape.'

There was a pause. Then: 'Why did you bring us evening dresses? We never go out at night.'

'Those aren't evening dresses. They are nightgowns.' I could sense her growing astonishment.

'I have never seen clothes like that. I was only three when the revolution came,' she said, almost apologetically.

Poor woman, she was in her fifties and her lot had been only sadness and privation. I was filled with gratitude that I had escaped her fate.

Before I left to return to England her husband Nicolai took me aside. 'Tell me,' he said, 'those nightgowns you gave to my wife. Who wears them in the West? Film stars, or who?'

'My dear Nicky,' I replied, 'Everybody does. Really.'

He shook his head. 'How extraordinary!' he muttered. But I knew he believed me.

I was told that the service in the café downstairs was much quicker than in the hotel restaurant, so one morning when I was in a hurry I went down there for my breakfast. The doorman was turning people away, but I showed my foreign passport to prove that I was a hotel guest and was shown to an empty seat at a table for two. I ordered by breakfast in Russian, to the apparent surprise of my table companion. He struck up a conversation almost at once.

'Are you Russian?'

'No, I am a British tourist.'

'But your Russian is perfect!'

I laughed. 'You are flattering me. You haven't heard enough yet!'

He was interested to know where I came from, how I had learnt Russian, how long was I staying? I decided to give him half-truths only, and explained that my parents had lived in Russia for a while before World War I, that I had had a Russian nanny and had learnt Russian as a child. I told him that I lived in London and travelled quite a lot because I dealt in antiques, and I had come to revisit his country because I remembered it so vividly from my childhood. This brought the inevitable question, 'How do you like Russia?'

After only four days in Moscow, how was I to answer him? How could I tell this amiable stranger that I found his country devastated, poor, oppressed and spoiled beyond belief? That I still loved the people, still felt some sense of belonging, but that the country was not the same, that the beauty had gone out of it. How could I tell him that?

'I find that it is not the country that my *niania* taught me to know and to love. She was deeply religious and took me to all kinds of divine services. Now I find that most of those beautiful churches are empty shells. Why have you spoiled such a national heritage, and such a beautiful one?'

'I agree,' he answered. 'But we are beginning to restore our monuments. Of course we should have done it ten years ago, but then we had other priorities.'

'Since we are having such a friendly talk, may I also ask you a few questions?' I asked. He smiled. 'How is it that you, a Russian, are sitting here in this privileged place reserved for foreigners, drinking tea and eating caviar at nine o'clock in the morning?'

I must have embarrassed him, but he did not hesitate. 'My office is just around the corner. If I'm not feeling too good I sometimes come in here and have something.' I thought it a poor explanation, and he quickly changed the subject. 'You told me you deal in antiques. You must live with beautiful things.'

'I make a point of it.'

'That is what I miss. Me, I'm a university graduate, I've a responsible job. Most of us are graduates now, but we've no culture. The State has educated us, yet the things we should have learnt on our mothers' knees have been denied to us. I long for culture, but how am I to acquire it?'

'You should travel,' I suggested. 'There's nothing like it.'

'But I do,' he said. 'All over Russia. I have to recruit men. It's very difficult. Often I have to offer perks in order to recruit them.'

I did not ask him what work it was and he didn't volunteer any more information. 'You should go abroad,' I continued, tongue in cheek. 'You should go to Italy if you're looking for culture.'

He didn't answer. Maybe he thought me naïve or ignorant, but I pressed on to see what he would say. 'You could come to London. I will invite you.'

After a moment's hesitation he looked me straight in the eye and said 'We are prisoners in our own country. We are only allowed out on special missions.'

I tried to look surprised. I hope I succeeded. 'I thought communism brought you freedom?' I said. But I warmed to him, because he had been honest with me, and I felt that many things had remained unsaid, so I was not surprised when, next morning, he was waiting when I came down for breakfast. 'I hoped I should see you again before you went. When are you leaving?'

'In about half an hour.'

'But you are coming back to Moscow?'

I nodded.

'Could we see each other then? Would you dine with me?' He was very pressing.

'With pleasure, but how are we going to find each other?'

To find someone in a Russian hotel is a *tour de force*, unless you know their room number and the name of the hotel, and both are only revealed by Intourist when you actually arrive. The stranger was well aware of this. 'I'll give you my telephone number,' he suggested. 'My name is Alexei Ivanovich.'

I made a note in my diary, but I realised that he hadn't given me his surname. 'Who shall I ask to speak to?'

'Just ask for Alexei Ivanovich. In any case, it's a private line, only I will answer.'

We said goodbye, and I left, wondering whether he was an *agent provocateur* planted there to quiz unsuspecting tourists, or a man who wanted to escape to the West and was trying perhaps to obtain some information or addresses? I shall, of course, never know. I made no attempt to contact him, and avoided that restaurant in future.

CHAPTER FIFTEEN

Our tour was to Moscow, Vladimir Suzdal, Pakoff and Leningrad. The Intourist brochure specified tourist, first-class and de luxe classes of accommodation. We had booked de luxe, which cost an extra £6 for the ten days. The tour price included absolutely everything, and we soon discovered that the food vouchers were more than adequate. The menus in the restaurants listed a large number of dishes, but most of them were unavailable. The food generally available, with local variations, consisted of bread, butter, tea, soured cream, cucumber salad, sturgeon, *blinis*, herring, chicken cutlets, *kefit*, cheesecakes and milk. Cheesecakes, which became Agnes' mainstay, were only served at breakfast time. *Blinis* for some reason always arrived cold. We never saw green vegetables, and though strawberries were in season we saw them only once, in Vladimir. We had brought lemons; we found out later that they were strictly forbidden, so it was lucky for us that the Customs men hadn't spotted them. At the restaurant at the Metropole Martine ordered apricots, seeing them listed on the menu under *Fruit*. The waiter asked how many we wanted, explaining that they were served by weight, and brough us a 1lb bag of green and quite uneatable apricots. Yet the markets were full of fruit, which somehow never reached the hotels.

When we ordered a meal all the food was brought together— the soup, the salads, the main dish, the ice cream and the tea. You had to choose between letting the ice-cream melt and having the soup while it was hot, or eating the ice-cream while the soup grew cold.

Once I saw an elderly American couple order tea at a nearby table. Two glasses were brought, in the Russian manner, but the couple, who no doubt were thirsty, asked for more. The waitress went off with a very bad grace, mumbling 'Why can't they ask for everything at once?'

You had to fight for everything you wanted, although as

tourists we were privileged. They never refused our requests, but time did not exist; you might be told to 'Come back in half an hour,' only to find that Maria Ivanovna had gone off duty and Olga Petrovna knew nothing about it. We were well treated by their standards. We were a 'tour of four', and were taken on all the excursions, in two taxis where one would have been enough. There was an Intourist guide in each taxi. An American girl, who was a 'tour of one', cottoned on to us because she was lonely.

As we waited for the Intourist guide who was to accompany us to the station and to the train to Vladimir, the next stage of our journey, a peculiar 'half-starved intellectual' type of young man introduced himself as our guide and asked if we spoke Italian. 'No-one understands Italian in Moscow,' he said. 'I can say what I like!' He sounded so defiant that I felt nervous and avoided his company by going in the second taxi. At the station he had difficulty in finding the train scheduled for us. The one at the time indicated was 'hard seats only', and our guide was indignant and apologetic. He passed a few uncomplimentary remarks about the Intourist organisation, but we were secretly pleased at the chance of a bit of local colour and of travelling with ordinary Russians. He installed us in a carriage, wished us a safe journey, and disappeared. We were on our own for the first time, and delighted. We decided to speak French or English but certainly no Russian, so that we could overhear the remarks made by the other occupants of the carriage.

We were the objects of much discreet curiosity. Our travelling companions were ordinary people who had possibly never met foreigners before. They discussed our clothes, our shoes, our bags and our gloves, and came to the conclusion that we must be very rich. We, for our part, were very impressed by the cleanliness of the carriage. The floors were spotless, there were none of the sunflower seeds which used in the past to litter all public places in Russia, and our fellow-travellers were orderly and well behaved. Most had bundles with them, some even had livestock. A boy of about seven had a pair of squirrels in a cage. He was the only child in the compartment; we had noticed how few children we had seen, and discovered that there are few large families in Russia today. The climate of fear is still such that people are reluctant to bring children into the world, in spite of the efforts of the State to encourage them to have more children. Mary produced some snapshots of her grandchildren to show us, and explained to her neighbour, using sign language, that she had eight of them. The woman immediately relayed this information to the other travellers:

'Fancy, this foreign woman has eight grandchildren, and we, when we have one or two we're happy!'

The train rattled on, passing endless forests of white birch and open country full of wild flowers. There were none of the villages I remembered, with tiny *isbouchkis* (wooden shacks) and a few hens scratching in the yard or a cow or two grazing peacefully nearby. Presumably all this had been replaced by the *kholhoz* (collective farm). After three and a half hours of travelling through this kind of landscape we arrived in Vladimir, sore from sitting so long on the wooden seats, and were met by a beautiful well-bred girl from Intourist who spoke flawless French. How had such a creature escaped the net, how had she been allowed to survive in a country where class is anathema?

A friend in London had warned me to be prepared for the worst as far as accommodation in Vladimir was concerned. It was therefore a pleasant surprise to be driven to an attractive three-storey house and shown into the best apartment (Russian style) we were to have during our whole tour. There was a large double bedroom, a drawing-room with a television set, a dining-room with a vast, old-fashioned refrigerator as a centrepiece, and a bathroom where, admittedly, the bath-towels had seen better days. This apartment was for Mary and I; Agnes and Martine had a similar one, while a third went to a Canadian professor who had somehow become attached to our tour. The house had obviously been privately owned at one time; all the linen bore embroidered initials and there were a few antiques that must have been overlooked by the looters.

In the dining-room downstairs the Canadian professor, a charming woman in her thirties, joined us. We were the only guests, and we were given a very cordial reception. Here we were given initialled damask napkins, where previously we had had to make do with paper napkins cut into four, or sometimes eight, pieces,

It was still light when we finished dinner, so Agnes, Martine and I decided to have a look at the town. As we left the hotel a rather large couple stopped to stare at us. The man pointed a fat finger at us: '*Anglichani, anglichani!*' he said, smiling to reveal

162

a mouth full of gold teeth. (In the Soviet Union you pay for gold teeth, silver ones are provided free by the State. This man's wife, I noticed, had silver teeth!)

'Yes, you are right,' I replied; 'We are English, but I happen to speak your language as well as you do!'

He was obviously impressed. 'How can that be?' he asked.

'We are very clever in the West,' I replied, and immediately saw that not only did he believe me but that they were both quite impressed.

'Where are you going?' he asked.

'We are going to have a look at your town before it gets dark.'

'Can we show it to you?'

I jumped at his proposal and explained it to Agnes and Martine who followed while I walked between the Russian couple. He did most of the talking, told me he was a physical culture instructor (he looked like a weightlifter) and—like most people in the Soviet Union—was a university graduate.

We came to a church standing in an old burial ground. Like most Russian churches, it was just a shell; obviously no services had been held here for many years. I stopped to read an inscription when the man suddenly asked 'What is your name?'

'Call me Margarita Andreevna,' I replied.

'Well, Margarita Andreevna, he said, 'I want you to answer a few questions but first you must promise to do so truthfully and not give me any of your capitalist lies.'

I was furious. 'Look,' I said, 'I don't give a damn about your questions—it's you who wants to ask them. If you think I am a liar, don't ask. I know all I want to know and I am only interested in visiting your town.' My anger was genuine, and he softened his tone at once.

'Now, now, don't get mad,' he said soothingly.

'I am mad. If you want to talk, then let's trust each other. Otherwise we can just as well visit the place without you.'

At that, he started to put his questions:

'Where do you live?'

'In London.'

'How many square metres do you have?'

'I haven't the slightest idea. It's a small house.'

'How small?' he asked, pointing to a building about the size of Buckingham Palace. 'Like that?'

'Certainly not! I said small.'

'How many rooms?'

'Two bedrooms, two bathrooms, living-room, kitchen and hall.'

'How many square metres in all?'

I turned to Martine, who worked it out quickly in her head.

'But who lives in all that space?' he wondered.

'I told you. I do. And sometimes relatives or friends come to stay.' I could see he thought something was wrong somewhere.

'How many hours of physical instruction do you have in schools?'

Martine, who had just left school, told him; it apparently was about what he expected, because he muttered 'Same as we have.' Perhaps I was really telling the truth!

'Have you got a car?' (Few private citizens then had cars in Russia.)

'Yes.' I realised that they were quite impressed by now.

'What do you do for a living?'

'I buy and sell antiques.'

'For the government?'

'No,' I replied, laughing. 'For myself.'

Both the man and his wife looked astonished and incredulous. Turning to me abruptly, he said 'Do you know what you are? You're a speculator, and in this country you would be shot at once, against that wall over there!'

I translated this last remark to Agnes and Martine, who burst out laughing. The couple could see that we were genuinely amused, which puzzled them even more.

We were just passing a large building in the Palladian style. They had volunteered to show us the sights, so I asked them what it was.

'It's nothing,' said Gold Teeth.

'What do you mean? It must be something. What is it?' I insisted.

The woman replied 'It's some kind of government building.' Slightly embarrassed, they both began to walk a little faster.

Next day I discovered that it was actually the local head-quarters of the KGB, and when we returned to London I found that at the time the two dissident writers, Bukovsky and Amalrik, had been imprisoned there. Our two companions, like most other

Russians, avoided such places, trying neither to think nor to talk about them. Evidently years of executions, arrests, betrayals by relatives or children, years of fear, have left their marks. Often when trying to trace old friends—usually without success—I have found people have either 'forgotten' what happened to them or will not talk about it. They do not trust each other; in fact often they seemed to trust me, a foreigner who was just passing through, more than their own kin.

These two strangers were now quite friendly and unafraid. 'Look at my wife's cardigan,' said the man. 'Go on, touch it! It's imported,' he said proudly. 'How much would it cost in England?'

'About three pounds,' I guessed.

'How much is that in roubles?'

'It depends on the rate of exchange. Officially, about four-fifty roubles.'

He looked at me accusingly, obviously displeased. 'We paid eighteen roubles,' he said, and turned to his wife for confirmation.

'That's not my fault,' I replied. 'Nothing to do with me!'

'Could anyone open a clothes shop in England?' he went on.

'Of course, why not?'

'But how would they get hold of the goods?'

'They'd buy them from a wholesaler.'

This was completely beyond them and I went into great detail explaining the intricacies of Western life.

It was growing dark by this time. We were in a deserted alley, where the evening air smelt damp and sweet. Suddenly I heard Martine gasp and, turning round, I saw a militiaman by her side. He must have overtaken us silently in the dark, and could not fail to have heard some of our conversation. The two Russians became absolutely terrified and started trembling all over. The militiaman gave them a long, hard look as he overtook us, and the woman, almost hysterical with fear, kept saying 'Shut up! shut up! You saw who it was! You shouldn't have asked such questions!' Her husband was pretty panicky too, and before I could say any more they had melted away into the night. Their fear had communicated itself to us, and it was our turn to feel guilty and nervous. Martine grabbed my arm, crying: 'We'll all get arrested in this damned country, you'll see!' as we hurried back to our hotel.

The beautiful Intourist guide who had met us at the station was standing at the door of the hotel, gazing sadly in front of her.

'Good evening,' I said. 'I see you are enjoying the lovely soft air.'

'That is all I have left,' she said, very quietly.

Needless to say, although Vladimir is a very small town, we never caught sight of our two guides again.

CHAPTER SIXTEEN

Next morning I asked a waitress if it was possible to attend an Orthodox religious service in Vladimir. She gave me an address and said she thought there was a service that night, and so at six o'clock that evening Agnes and I set out to investigate.

We found the church. It was small, with rusty gates and beggars at the door, and inside the service had already started. There were about fifty people in the congregation, mostly old women wearing headscarves, and a choir which consisted of a middle-aged man with a beard, three old women and a girl of about fourteen. The simple service was warm and strangely moving, full of mystical fervour. The old women crossed themselves as if trying to tear their hearts out, and banged their foreheads on the stone floor. Tears ran down their wrinkled faces, Slav faces that I knew so well—familiar, kind faces which I had now caught unawares, a suffering humanity that I had sensed from the beginning and now discovered for myself.

On our right a man wearing a mackintosh of a type worn by countless Russians was praying with the special fervour which one only sees in Russia. His face was deathly white, his eyes closed; he clasped and unclasped his hands to make the sign of the cross, but really he was oblivious of everything. Occasionally he wiped away a tear that trickled down his face. We sensed his tragedy so strongly that we felt compelled to pray with him. Tired after our day's outing, we were transported into a spiritual world where we would gladly have stood next to that stranger for ever. And yet, not having been through such sufferings ourselves, we could only guess at the misery which had brought forth such fervour.

After this experience we attended religious services whenever we got a chance, partly perhaps out of a kind of bravado, but also from a feeling of compassion for the oppressed. We wanted to show that we were on their side. Once we even followed a motley procession on its way to venerate the Cross. All eyes were on us—we were so obviously foreigners—but at least our gestures stopped the Intourist guides from showing their usual contempt for religion.

'Are you of the Orthodox religion?' one of them asked.

'No, only Christians,' I replied.

On the ramparts of the city of Vladimir, the guide stopped to give an account of the history of the place. Nearby a couple of children were painting in bright oils (I noticed that painting and drawing are extremely common in Russia.) They were with a youngish, rather bedraggled man I assumed was their father. He kept looking at us furtively, trying to follow the guide's narrative in English. Suddenly, gesticulating wildly, he shouted in Russian: 'Don't believe what she tells you, it's all lies, don't believe a word of it!'

Continuing to shout abuse, he walked away, swaying drunkenly and cursing the regime. '*In vino veritas,*' I thought. The guide pretended not to hear, and luckily there was no-one else around.

Incidents like these are quite common, and of course they do not matter if the tourists can't understand Russian. If the tourists ask questions, they are often told anything but the truth, and I amused myself by providing authentic translations whenever the opportunity arose. During a bus tour of Leningrad we listened to a history of the revolution which stressed Lenin's part but missed out Trotsky, who has, I imagine, been left out of the Russian history books. The guide also skipped over Stalin, apparently not then quite restored to favour. We happened to be passing some houses built during Stalin's rule—a mass builder as well as a mass murderer, his style is easily recognisable—so I asked the guide: 'Weren't those houses built when Stalin was in power?'

'Yes,' replied the guide, and changed the subject, but I persisted: 'What about Trotsky? You haven't told us what happened to him.'

An American sitting next to me smiled. 'Are you doing it on purpose, ma'am?' he asked.

From Vladimir we were to travel by train to Pskoff, leaving at 6pm that evening. We were escorted to our sleeping compartment, which was still locked, so we waited for the attendant. She was a peasant woman of uncertain age, and when she appeared she banged with all her might on the locked door. A man in army uniform, covered in gold braid and decorations, emerged from the compartment and with him a smell of putrid tobacco. It was so smoky you could hardly see in.

'We have booked a non-smoker,' I said to the attendant in Russian. She turned on the army man: 'Can't you see these are foreign ladies? How dare you use filthy tobacco where they are supposed to travel?' She showed little respect for his rank, called him by every swear word in the dictionary (and a few that probably aren't included!), and the man sneaked off making himself as small as possible. She opened the windows, emptied all the ashtrays and used some kind of smoke-extractor, grumbling all the time about 'the kind of people who use the railways nowadays'. She was the real Russian peasant, the salt of the earth and no nonsense! We settled in and she brought us some tea. There was no food to be had either on the train or in the station, and we had not eaten since morning. The old woman commiserated, explained that when we arrived at Pskoff at five o'clock that morning we would be able to get some food and, obviously delighted to be able to speak in Russian to a foreigner, sat down on the lower couch and began to talk.

She was very ignorant. She had no idea where England or France were, and when we told her they were only about three and a half hours' flying-time away, she remarked that she 'didn't know they were next door'. She came from Leningrad, had been through the blockade and had lost both her sons in the war. She talked about the terrible cold and hunger she had been through.

'I saw people in the streets stop walking and fall down dead,' she said. 'Next door to me lived an old man with his daughter and her two children. Her husband was fighting in the front line. They all died from hunger and were half eaten by the rats. I helped to drag their bodies out into the street, but they lay there quite a while in the snow because there weren't enough trucks to pick up all the dead.'

Like many illiterates she had a wonderful memory. Sometimes she rabbled out passages from the Bible, sometimes she told us about herself: 'I retired from the railways at fifty-five. I've got a pension of sixty-five roubles a month, and my lodging allocation, but what can I do, sitting at home all the time? So I went back to work. I love trains.' She was a rich woman, she said, what

L   169

with her wages and her pension. 'I've got everything I want, even a television set. But I'm fed up with watching it, there's far too much propaganda.'

'Propaganda, propaganda, there's nothing else,' she grumbled. 'They even told us there was a man in space! Why, the other day they had the nerve to announce that men had actually landed on the moon! Of course, I didn't believe a word of it! I know it's all propaganda.'

Pskoff, which is where Nicholas II abdicated, proved to be a dismal town; the October Hotel was a very gloomy spot, and the porter, with a cigarette dangling from his lips and his cap on the back of his head, was apparently slightly drunk. It wasn't easy to persuade him to carry our luggage to our rooms, which were extremely spartan, with no hot water, no bathroom and no WC.

We were hungry and miserable, and we longed for hot baths. The woman at the desk promised to bring us some tea at once, and suggested that we should sleep until breakfast time and sort it all out with Intourist then. But when we went down for breakfast we found that the dining-room was closed. The same woman directed us to a small café at the end of a corridor, full of work-men eating indescribable food. The buns on display were stale and fly-ridden. We sat down to see what the service was like (we had after all paid for a 'de-luxe' tour) and after a few seconds the girl at the counter yelled 'If you want something, queue up!'

I chose not to understand and we left without a word. The Intourist office had just opened. I went up to the young man behind the desk.

'Why do our rooms have no bathrooms? Where can we have breakfast? I demand first-class accommodation!'

He consulted his list. 'In Pskoff you are only tourist class. You have been given the right accommodation,' he said.

I asked to see the list, and sure enough it was marked 'de luxe' everywhere except in Pskoff, where 'tourist class' was underlined in red! It turned out that this was because there was no better accommodation in the town. The young man was very apologetic, and when I told him that the dining-room was closed he opened it and served us himself. As we found so often, the Russians could scarcely have been kinder or more pleasant, but all their organisations seemed to be perfectly chaotic.

The hotel was used a great deal by local officials who came and went in large, Russian-made cars with military chauffeurs. They reminded me of Chicago gangsters of the prohibition era; they were by no means prepossessing. Neither were the 'guests' occupying the other rooms in the hotel; as we were the only women staying there, we hardly dared to go to the loo alone, there were so many gorilla-like characters in the corridors!

But the countryside around Pskoff was beautiful, as we saw the next day when there was an excursion to Pecheri Monastery, some eighty miles away. Our drivers were two young men to whom a car was still an exciting new toy. They took short cuts whenever the chance arose, careering across the fields while we hung on for dear life.

The monastery was magnificent, especially by contrast with the drabness of Pskoff. A niche in the entrance was decorated with a painting of the Virgin, and the inside walls of the courtyard were covered with paintings of saints. There were no statues of Lenin, no political slogans; we were surprised by how beautiful it was, and how well tended. It was the first such place we had seen in Soviet Russia. The guide explained that 'In the war everything here was looted by the Germans, with the connivance of the monks. Now other monks have replaced them, and have repainted and restored it all.' He didn't go into detail about the fate of the former monks!

One of the monks took us to see the crypt. We followed with lighted candles, reading the inscriptions. I noted that Pushkin's family had all been buried here. We didn't learn as much about the monastery as we could have wished because the monk was very careful what he said. He showed us the vegetable garden and told us that the monastery was completely self-supporting. He pointed out the orchard, where the trees and bushes were laden with fruit. We had seen almost no fresh fruit in Russia and, perhaps seeing the longing in our eyes, he picked some raspberries for us.

As we made our way back to the car a service was just finishing and a crowd had gathered outside the door of the church. I was surprised to see our driver among them, and when we got back in the car he handed me a piece of paper.

'You may be interested in this. I took it for my granny but you can read it if you like.'

It was a religious poem and my first encounter with the *Samizdat*. 'Where did you get it?' I asked.

'One of the monks gave it to a woman and she passed it on to me. I was lucky.'

'Why?'

'Because the monk knew I was with Intourist; he would never have dared to give it to me.'

'Why did you take it?'

'I told you. For my granny. She's illiterate, but I can read it to her.'

'It's very beautiful,' I said. 'Do you think I could copy it?'

'Keep it,' he replied with typical Russian generosity.

'No, no; your granny needs it more than I do. I have my own faith. Are you a believer?'

'I believe in Lenin.'

'But Lenin was only a man. Surely that's not enough? Surely you believe in something higher?'

'What's the difference whether I do or don't? I've got a good job. If I start going to church, that will be a black mark against my name. I could lose my job; it isn't worth it.'

There was no excursion arranged for the next afternoon, so the Canadian professor suggested that we should all go to look at a church with some interesting bas reliefs of musical instruments, which had something to do with her research work. We took a taxi, and I sat next to the driver as usual, in order to be able to ask a lot of questions.

This particular driver was a short, tough-looking man of between fifty or sixty, a remnant of the 'lost generation', millions of whom perished during the war or in Stalin's concentration camps. I was particularly keen to talk with him for this reason, but at first he was not at all communicative. He seemed very much a 'party liner'. We drove through a deserted countryside, field after field with not a cow or a sheep in sight, and he explained that the peasants were moving into the towns and the rural areas were losing their populations. 'The government has now realised the problem,' he said, 'and has started to give the workers small allotments that they can build a house on. This then becomes their own property, which they can sell or bequeath to anyone they like.'

172

To me this sounded like a return to some form of capitalism. The driver did not disagree with me, but went on to extol Lenin. 'Had Lenin lived,' he said, 'things would have been very different, very much better.'

The church we were visiting was abandoned, and in the field was a bench where there had once been a footpath to the church. I sat down and beckoned to him to join me. I told him about some of the many things I remembered from my childhood in Russia. 'I have always wanted to come back,' I told him, 'but this is no longer the Russia I loved.'

I think he could sense that I was upset by what I had seen in his country after my long exile, and could tell that my love of Russia was sincere, because his whole expression began to soften.

'I know how you must feel,' he replied. 'I, too, was a small child when the revolution broke out. My parents, I think, must have been well-to-do people, as far as I can recollect. They were killed. I don't know how, or where, in fact I don't even know what they were called. My little sister and I were suddenly alone, roaming the woods, eating wild berries and whatever we could find. At first we cried a lot, but we got used to it and began to live like two little animals. We were rounded up, of course, in the end, like all the other *beprizorny*, and after that I never saw my little sister again. I was put in an orphanage, and at the age of fifteen I was drafted into the Red Army.'

I suddenly remembered my little friend Bunchy, and how a soldier had taken her away.

'I fought in the war,' he continued, 'and was decorated. After the war I got married. Our only daughter was musical, but this is a small town and there are no facilities for that, so the State decreed that she must go to a technical college. We weren't given any choice; we never are. Now she is far away and we won't see her for two years. Do you wonder that there are a lot of drunks in this country? What is there left? They have made cattle out of our women, they have to work like animals, they don't even have time to wash. Our children are no longer our own, the State takes them over, and so you come home to an empty hearth and then you go out to get drunk and forget.'

When we got back to the hotel there were eight roubles on the clock. 'We are in a communist country,' I said, 'and therefore I know that it is not customary to tip. But we have talked as friends and I would like to show you my appreciation.'

'Yes,' he answered, 'I suppose I should refuse. But anything you care to give me I shall gratefully accept.'

CHAPTER SEVENTEEN

We left Pskoff without regret, and continued to Leningrad, where we found the atmosphere much less oppressive. The people did not seem quite so harassed.

The taxi-driver who took us to the Hermitage asked gaily 'Where to, *Mesdames*?'

'How nice to be called "Mesdames",' I said.

'Well, I can tell just by looking that you must be returning to our country after many years. You probably realise that I have not always been a taxi-driver. . . . But my son is all right. He'll be a big man one day,' he said, with great pride.

We were very impressed by the young people we met in Russia. They were so well behaved, so studious and idealistic. They knew nothing about Stalin, or about the famines, the fear and the persecution that had haunted Russia, and they were very proud of their country. Unfortunately I wasn't allowed to meet the sons or daughters of some of my acquaintances. Miloucha had explained that 'My son has married a communist girl. She's quite nice and he's happy with her, but what have we got in common?'

They all seem to believe that it is dangerous for their children to meet foreigners. Once, in a Leningrad hotel, I complimented a waitress on her service. She was very flattered. 'Several foreign ladies have told me so,' she said. She told me that one American woman had always asked for her. 'She said I knew exactly how she liked her eggs done.' When she went back to America she had sent the waitress a postcard. 'I didn't sleep at nights for quite a while after that! I have a husband and three lovely children; I want to go on living!'

'Why?' I asked. 'What harm is there in getting a postcard from abroad?'

'I don't know. I never ask why any more. I just don't want trouble, that's all.'

I gave her a cheap scarf and she blushed with pleasure and thanked me effusively. I felt like Dr Livingstone distributing beads in darkest Africa. . . .

Our hotel in Leningrad was a modern skyscraper which was starting to fall to pieces already, though it was only about a year old. When we were leaving for London I met a very old American who had stayed at the same hotel, and as he was having a bit of trouble I went across and offered my services as an interpreter. Afterwards I asked him what had brought him to Russia.

'Madam,' he replied solemnly, 'Adventure!'

I had to laugh. 'We stayed at the same hotel in Leningrad,' I said. 'You should have tried the restaurant on the eighteenth floor. The service was quite good.' (Which was quite true, though the parquet floor was badly warped by rain leaking through the roof.)

'Madam,' said the American, 'I wouldn't chance an eighteenth floor in the Soviet Union.'

We were scheduled to return from Leningrad to Moscow and catch our London connection on 21 July. But when we asked for our tickets the Intourist official told us that these were for the 22nd. I had to go through the whole business about our changed dates several times, and there seemed to be so much red tape involved that I thought we should never sort it out. But we did eventually, and had our first experience of Russian internal flights. I can't say we were very impressed, but we landed exactly on time, and on the pretext of going to the toilets I slipped out through a side entrance and phoned Mitia. 'We'll be at the Metropole again,' I told him. But when we arrived at the Metropole and the Intourist guide handed over the documents, we found that for some reason our booking hadn't been made. We weren't on any of their lists and that was that. After the usual pandemonium and frantic telephoning, someone said 'Take them to the Rossia Hotel.'

'We're not going there,' I said. 'It isn't de luxe, because there are bugs there. British tourists have warned us.'

Our Canadian friend had shown us where she had been bitten and said she had been eaten alive! The two women in the Intourist office looked sheepish and admitted that they had heard rumours about the bugs; satisfied, I returned to my armchair and waited for results. Finally they decided to send us to the

National Hotel. We were given two double rooms on different floors, and as soon as we had settled in I telephoned Mitia. He was with me in ten minutes.

Soon afterwards Nicolai and Miloucha arrived, carrying several strange-looking parcels. I had mentioned in passing some of the Russian foods I was specially fond of, and they brought the lot— black bread, home-made jam, special *blini* flour, and other delicacies. Then Nicolai presented me with a large parcel tied up with real silk ribbon—a survivor from the old days.

'We want you to take this out,' he said.

Watched by them all I unwrapped it, revealing a lovely, precious ikon. I was overwhelmed. 'You can't give me this!' I protested. I knew how much it was worth, and how poor they all were. They could have lived well on the proceeds for months.

'Look, you must understand,' said Nicolai. 'It's no good to us. We cannot sell it, we can't display it, we're not even supposed to own it. Miloucha has been hiding it for fifty years. It's the only thing of any value we have. It's for you—a souvenir from us all.'

'I will treasure it, you can be sure.' I hugged them all in turn, deeply touched. We had spoken in whispers, afraid of being overheard.

Anxious to talk freely, we went out into the streets. They were eager to hear about our travels, about Leningrad, Vladimir, Pskoff. Even to travel between cities in Russia, they needed permits, so secondhand impressions were better than none at all. They clustered round me on a bench we found on one of the boulevards, anxious to hear everything I had to tell.

'Did you visit the Winter Palace? What did you think of it?'

'Frankly, I was disappointed.'

They all wanted to know why.

'I suppose it was the dinginess. The parquet floors are beautiful, made of countless different types of wood, and yet people are practically allowed to walk on them in hobnailed boots! Visitors sit on the imperial furniture, bits of veneer are missing, objects are chipped or cracked. It's pure vandalism! You've got some wonderful treasures, but they aren't being properly displayed or looked after, or even properly cleaned. They are all just there.' They listened in silence. 'Everything in Peter the Great's room is made of silver, but it's so black it looks like wrought iron! I even asked one of the attendants why it was in such a state, but his explanation wouldn't hold water anywhere. He said if people didn't know it was silver, it wouldn't get pinched!'

'So you're disappointed?' said Mitia

'Yes, and no. But it's a shame to see everything uncared for.'

'Give us time,' said Nicolai. 'We have been so ravaged by war and we help so many underdeveloped countries, we can't do everything at once. You must look at our achievements. Our education is first-class; everyone in Russia goes to university.'

'I agree, it is admirable, and much better than it was under the tsars, when most people couldn't read or write. But with so many people educated at university, who is going to be left to do the plumbing, the building and other essential jobs?'

'What don't you like here?' said Nicolai. 'Why do you keep saying that you live in a different world? We've got everything now.'

'What everything?' I retorted. 'What are you talking about? When did you eat fresh fish last? You told me yourself you haven't eaten it for several years.'

'Ah, but in two years' time we will have it.'

Now Mitia laughed. 'You've been saying that for the last twenty-five years!'

They continued to argue with me and among themselves, trying to unravel what it was I found so different.

'All right,' I said. 'One word will cover it. In England, I can go into the park, mount a soap-box and scream whatever I like at the top of my voice and nobody will touch me. The word is "Freedom".'

'Oh, that!' said Nicolai, with a sigh. 'We've forgotten what that word means!'

Unconsciously, we had raised our voices. Mitia made a sign to silence us. 'Don't speak so loud, they may hear us!'

'Who?' I asked. 'And how could they, anyway?'

'There are special devices that can pick up conversations several kilometres away,' explained Nicolai. 'It's dangerous.'

'Look, Nicolai, that's just fear talking. With a population of nearly nine million in this city alone, how could they possibly pick up a conversation on a park bench? You're so used to living in a police state, you see bogeymen everywhere.' But I convinced no-one.

Nicolai returned to the subject of the ikon.

'I won't be easy until you have got it out of the country. You have already been voicing your opinions loud and clear. Suppose they find the ikon?'

'So what?'

'You don't understand. There may be all sorts of unpleasantness. They may detain you. They can do anything they want. You'd better pass the blame on to me. Give them my name and say it was a present from me.'

For a moment I didn't grasp his meaning. When I did I got quite angry. 'You can think again!' I answered. 'I'll tell you what I'll say to them if they dare to stop me. I'll say that I am a Christian and have come to Russia with my ikon and that I'm jolly well going out with it again. That I pray in front of it every day and always have done, and that it's none of their business. I'm certainly not going to get you mixed up in it!'

The conversation drifted to lighter subjects—they asked about prices, particularly of the various things I had brought with me. Miloucha looked at my raincoat. 'How much does a coat like that cost?' she wanted to know.

'I'll give it to you before I leave. I can buy another one, they aren't expensive.' She smiled gratefully.

It was late, and we were due to leave the next day. It was time for them to be going home, but we arranged to meet the next day for the last goodbyes. I had a lot of vouchers left, so I asked them to lunch, thinking that it would be a pleasant way of using up all the vouchers.

Mitia came early, with his girlfriend Olga, an attractive blonde with a beautiful figure and a ready smile. She was carrying a bunch of cornflowers—I think I had mentioned that they reminded me of my childhood—and when she saw Agnes she divided the bunch in two with a spontaneous gesture that I thought very attractive.

Both Nicolai and Mitia entered the restaurant with considerable aplomb; it was a luxurious place reserved for tourists and party members, and for years these two had either been penniless or in concentration camps. I insisted that they order anything they wanted, as the vouchers had all been paid for and would otherwise be wasted, and they took me at my word. They took a good half-hour over the caviar alone, until I began to wonder if

I should miss my plane. When I began to get a little fidgety, they apologised, explaining that they had to savour these delicacies, as they might never taste them again! We made plans for my next visit the following January, and talked of going skiing through the birch woods. I begged Mitia to try to trace some of my childhood friends before I returned, and then suddenly it was time for me to leave.

We had, as usual, two taxis to the airport, and mercifully we cleared the Customs without incident; but there was a hold-up over boarding cards, and a BOAC official had to be called to sort things out. As we climbed aboard the aircraft we were greeted by a smiling steward, who said: 'I am sure you could all do with a drink, ladies!' Never was a drink more welcome!

CHAPTER EIGHTEEN

The wave of depression which submerged me on my return to London was the strongest I have ever experienced. No subsequent visit has affected me in the same way. It is one thing to read of what is done behind the Iron Curtain, and quite another to meet those who have actually lived through those experiences. Neither could I understand how such lives could be sustained daily, nor even less the complexities of the Russian character. There seemed to be two people inside every one of them. One moment I felt that I could trust them implicitly, the next I had a feeling that they could just as easily betray me. And yet the charm, the kindness and the complete self-abnegation were all still there, especially if one caught them in their unguarded moments.

I came to the conclusion that I should go back on my own, now that I knew how things worked, and in the winter, a time of year that I loved, I would try to unravel the mystery of this new Russia where everything was one enormous contradiction.

The following November I received a letter from Mitia's girlfriend Olga, telling me that he had been taken ill at work and had been rushed to hospital, where the doctors had diagnosed a heart attack. She was visiting him as often as she could, and at the same time looking after his invalid wife. The letter was very brief, and it worried me considerably.

Some time before I had been introduced to a woman who was on leave in London from her work in a foreign embassy in Moscow. Helen was dedicated to Russia and the Russians, but felt that the régime left much to be desired; one of her greatest disappointments was that after six years she was still excluded from any closer relationships with the people of the country. Her only contacts were with the embassy and domestic staff, provided with the compliments of the KGB. She couldn't trust anyone and felt frustrated, and she wasn't entirely at ease in the diplomatic circles in which she was forced to move. She was a good-looking woman in her late thirties; I liked her direct manner, and our common interest in Russia created an immediate bond. She offered her help if ever I should need it.

I now took advantage of her generous offer, sending her a letter by diplomatic bag explaining Mitia's position in detail and asking her to get in touch with his brother. I also sent some roubles for the brother to pass on to Mitia, and begged her to be very careful so as not to compromise anyone. Eventually I heard that the money had reached Mitia.

In December I went to the London Intourist office to make arrangements for my next trip to Moscow. The tour that came nearest to suiting my timetable and my pocket was called 'Winter Theatre Festival', but the ten days of this tour were split up into three days in Moscow, four days in Leningrad and three days in Moscow again. (Privately I suspect that this is a deliberate policy designed to prevent tourists from making contacts with the Russian people.)

To my great surprise, when I asked Intourist whether I could stay in Moscow for the whole tour, giving my love of the Bolshoi as a pretext, they raised no objections. I insisted on confirmation of this in writing, they promised to obtain it, and so I booked there and then.

I arranged my packing so that, apart from things like toiletries, I could wear almost everything I should need, thus liberating two huge suitcases which I filled to overflowing with clothing for my friends. The final effect was rather startling; I was about fifteen pounds heavier and looked as if I was setting out for the North Pole. I also carried an enormous handbag into which I crammed the heavier articles, including forbidden literature. I planned to shed the heavy coat, the fur-lined boots, the jacket of my suit and two heavy sweaters as soon as I got aboard the plane. Luckily it was half empty, so I was able to overflow into the next seat. I sat back, closed my eyes and started going through my plans for the next ten days.

I had told my Russian friends when I should be arriving, and I had also informed Helen at her embassy in order to be sure of a diplomatic contact if anything went wrong.

It was cloudy all the way. The plane came down on tarmac surrounded by mountains of snow as far as the eye could see.

The hostess announced that the ground temperature was twenty-six below, at which I hastily put all my heavy clothes back on. I cleared the passport formalities, declared the amount of currency I was carrying and also such capitalistic attributes as my gold watch, wedding ring and a pair of gold ear-rings, and went to the Intourist office to ask for a taxi. A young man glanced at my name on my passport and called out to a tall, well-dressed man standing a few steps away. He told me he was Helen's chauffeur and would take me to my hotel, and picking up my two heavy cases he jumped the queue and I followed him.

'How long are you staying?' inquired the Customs man.

'Ten days,' I replied.

'Why have you so much luggage?'

I looked at him in surprise. 'But with your cold climate I need a lot of warm clothes. Besides, I like to change often.'

He made me open one of the cases, passed his hand over a thick layer of jumpers, and waved me on.

The chauffeur opened the back door of the waiting Volvo, but I insisted on sitting in the front next to him. I wasn't going to miss the chance of talking to a real live *tovarich* from the KGB. He told me his name was Ivan and that he had been driving Helen for the past two years. He hoped to have the opportunity of taking me to various places. Helen didn't use her car very much, so he could often be at my disposal. He struck me as a friendly, polite, diffident man, not at all as I should have imagined a KGB employee.

I asked him whether he smoked, partly to make conversation and partly because I had several cheap gas-lighters with me as presents, knowing them to be highly prized in Russia.

'Sometimes, when I am alone,' he answered. 'Never in front of ladies, in case it is unpleasant to them. You see, I am a "gentleman".'

I assured him that I didn't mind if he smoked, but he was adamant that being a gentleman prevented him from smoking in the presence of ladies. There was no point in telling him that I was no longer used to such consideration, but I was very amused at the fascination the word 'gentleman' had for this son of the proletariat.

At the Metropole Hotel he went to sort out my accommodation and insisted on carrying my luggage to my room, where we shook hands and I thanked him for his trouble. He said that he hoped we should shortly meet again.

Before I unpacked I went down to the Intourist office to collect various vouchers and theatre tickets. Several of the women there had been friendly the summer before, and they remembered my name and gave me the vouchers I would need for three days in Moscow. 'The rest will be given to you in Leningrad.'

'But I'm not going to Leningrad,' I protested. 'It's been arranged that I am spending the whole ten days in Moscow.'

'That is impossible,' they said.

'No it is not! I have a Telex from your people confirming it.'

'Can I see it?' She scrutinised it thoroughly and passed it to one of her colleagues. 'May we keep it?' she asked.

'Oh no!' I said firmly. 'You can show it to anyone you wish but I'm not going to part with it.'

After the usual telephone calls and consultations, I was eventually issued with vouchers for ten days. I heaved a sigh of relief and congratulated myself on my foresight.

On the last day of my first visit I had managed to trace a schoolfriend called Nastia. She lived in a communal apartment which she said was so squalid that she didn't want to show it to me, and anyway she didn't trust the people with whom she shared it. We had arranged that she should wait for me to telephone her at her daughter's flat, and by this method we arranged to meet around the corner outside the hotel.

I took off my hat and put on a Russian headscarf and, hoping I now looked like a Soviet citizen, picked up my case and marched brazenly past the usual desk with its woman floor-spy. Within minutes Nastia and I had met and were walking towards the nearest taxi-rank, where we found another of those long queues that are an indispensable feature of Soviet life. The suitcase was too heavy for us to consider taking the metro, and we were just wondering what to do when a man came up and asked us whether we wanted a lift.

'How much?' was my friend's instant reaction.

'Five roubles.'

It was an outrageous amount of money but I overruled my friend's objections. At the price at which I had obtained my currency five roubles was more than reasonable.

We had not been travelling long when we were stopped by

some traffic lights, and I noticed a girl on the other side waving frantically. Our driver jumped the lights with no more ado, and as he stopped in front of the girl we heard a police-whistle being blown. He opened the door for the girl and jumped out, not before warning all three of us to say that we knew him and were his co-workers in a certain organisation. There followed a lengthy discussion between him and the policeman, who frequently looked suspiciously in our direction.

'He'll have to square him with a couple of roubles,' said the girl laconically. She was right. A minute later the driver passed something to the policeman and hurried back, looking a bit annoyed.

When we reached her flat, Nastia's daughter was horrified when we told her about our adventure, but it was soon forgotten when we opened the case. They were both like children in front of their first Christmas tree. They tried everything on, asked if they could keep the case, and plied me with tea and hospitality.

When I finally managed to get away, they helped me to find a taxi and I sat next to the driver. It was snowing and a couple of youngsters down the road were sheltering, waiting for the last bus. The taxi driver, after asking my permission, pulled up and told them to jump in.

The two teenagers listened curiously to our conversation. Then the boy asked if I was a tourist. I nodded.

'Are you a millionairess, then?' he asked.

'What makes you say that?'

'You couldn't afford to come here otherwise,' he said.

'Not at all,' I replied. 'Coming to Russia is one of the cheapest holidays we Westerners can buy. And I'm not a millionairess, I work for my living.'

He was surprised. 'Then why can't we do the same and visit your country?' he asked.

I suggested that he ask someone better qualified to answer.

When we reached the hotel I took off my headscarf and put on my fur hat, which had attached to it a cashmere scarf with which I could completely hide my face from the cold. What with that, my long fur-lined coat and my high fur boots, I felt like an Arab woman. Thus disguised, with only my eyes visible, I mounted the steps of the Metropole Hotel, just as a large young man was coming down. He must have dined and wined well, for he was in very high spirits, even by Russian standards. In the most atrocious French he greeted me with 'Bonsoir, jolie Madame!' and before I realised what was happening his strong arms had lifted me into the air as he gave a wild shriek of delight. He obviously thought he had found himself a dolly. As I flew through the air I recovered my wits enough to say 'Young man, you are fifty years too late!'

Luckily he didn't drop me and I landed safely. Hope never dies in the heart of a Russian, I thought. Perhaps that is how they have been able to survive so many horrors.

My room was unbearably hot, and it was impossible to turn off the radiator, so I was forced to open the window. I kept it open for the whole of my stay, much to the amazement of my chambermaid. The air was dry and crisp and the heating, which came from a central plant as electricity does with us, went on day and night, so I never felt the cold.

I went to bed relaxed and satisfied with my day. I had had a friendly reception, and I allowed myself to hope that things had become a little easier and that I would be able to understand a little more about the Soviet way of life. Next morning I arranged various appointments, falling more easily this time into the Russian habit of using the telephone frequently and at length, which is encouraged because the telephone is free for local calls. On my first visit I had been very dubious about phoning Mitia from the hotel, but he had reassured me and even taught me to dial direct.

Then I went down to the café for breakfast. I was spotted at once by a red-haired waitress who pointed to a table. When she had brought my breakfast the girl, who I shall call Tania, stood and chatted. In no time I had learnt that she lived with her mother, a daughter of seventeen, and a boy of four, on the outskirts of Moscow. There was no mention of a husband, and never likely to be. But she did tell me that it was difficult to bring up two children, and how hard she had to work to make ends meet. I gave her some chewing-gum and a pair of tights, which she gratefully stuffed into her pocket. At that moment we heard the sound of loud curses from the direction of the kitchen, followed by sobbing. Tania carried on talking, quite unperturbed, but I listened. Some woman was threatening another, calling her every kind of name and screaming that she would send her far away where work wouldn't be so easy. The sobbing and pleading grew louder, and I looked inquisitively at Tania.

'It's that fiend again,' she said. 'We have to be very careful when she's around.' At that moment the 'fiend' came into the restaurant and Tania promptly went on with her work. The 'fiend' was about forty-five, heavily built, with her black dyed hair in a huge tight knot on the top of her head. She was handsome in a Valkyrie sort of way, but her face had no softness or pity in it, and I imagine that wardresses in concentration camps often look something like her. As she swept out of the café, Tania whispered 'She's the head supervisor. We're all scared stiff of her.'

'Why, what can she do?'

'She can send you to a labour camp before you've had time to sneeze.'

'Surely that sort of thing is over?' I said.

'What d'you mean, over?' She gave me a condescending look. 'It goes on all the time. Only last week one of the waitresses was sent off because she spent five dollars at a *beriozka* shop. She had collected the foreign currency in small tips, but she copped it just the same.'

The girl who had felt the sharp end of the supervisor's tongue was clearing plates, her eyes puffed up from crying. I offered a silent prayer that, whatever she had done, she might get away with it, and I think she did, for I saw her several times after this.

I was prepared to consolidate my useful contact with Tania by giving her presents. My large black bag, which went with me everywhere, contained small gifts and works by Soljenitzin, Pasternak, Mandelstamm and others, all forbidden in the Soviet Union and printed in pocket editions in Paris. For obvious reasons I dared not leave it in my room and was simply awaiting the opportunity of distributing its contents. I gave presents to people like Tania, forbidden literature to those who sought enlightenment. With the zeal of a missionary, I was prepared to go to almost any length if it could bring a little relief or happiness to the drab lives of such people. With roubles purchased in London at fifteen to the pound instead of the miserable four-twenty-five the Russians were prepared to give, I never missed an opportunity to have tea or ice-cream in the café and a talk to Tania. And it was Tania who made the first approach that led to our own 'black market'. 'My daughter is pestering me for a piece of jewellery sold at the *beriozka* shop. If I gave you foreign currency, could you buy it?' she asked. I was only too pleased to do it, of course.

'How about supplying me with a pot of caviar for roubles?' I asked. 'Have you got a jar?' she asked. Seeing my surprised look, she told me where I could buy suitable jars, and thereafter whenever Tania was on duty I could buy caviar by the pound in my own jars. It worked out at about three pounds fifty pence per pound, and it was very welcome when I took it to Russian friends.

Tania did so well out of these transactions that there was soon no caviar to be had in the entire Metropole Hotel. One day at lunch I sat at the same table as a French couple with whom I got into conversation. He was a director of Renault, and had come on a tour of inspection of the Renault plant in Moscow. When he heard that I spoke Russian, he suggested that I ask Tania why there was no caviar to be had at the Metropole when it seemed so plentiful elsewhere, little suspecting the irony of the situation.

'Has life in Russia always been so dreary?' he asked me.

I assured him that it had not; that, on the contrary, most foreigners had been devoted to Russia, and that in exile they had never quite reconciled themselves to the loss of the happiness they had experienced in Russia.

'The country must have changed a lot,' he said. 'Our workmen here are mostly French communists, and they nearly all dislike the place so much that they won't agree to their wives coming out to join them. I have to grant them leave of absence every now and then. When they return to France they get mad with their comrades who haven't been out here because they won't believe that the Soviet Union isn't paradise on earth.'

CHAPTER NINETEEN

Next morning at the Intourist office I told Maria Petrovna that I wanted to visit Zagorsk.

'Nothing easier,' she said. 'There are excursions every Tuesday.' But her optimism was unfounded; the only remaining Tuesday of my trip there was no trip to Zagorsk, and all my suggestions and stratagems met with excuses. In the end I was forced to take up Helen's offer of the loan of her car and her chauffeur Ivan, and a trip was fixed for the following Sunday. At the last moment Helen decided to come too.

The route to Zagorsk took us along the Leningrad road, but how different it was from our journeys to Himki along the same route fifty years ago! Now the friendly countryside was deserted, with only a police post every two or three miles where a militiaman would salute, note the car number and rush to his telephone, presumably to inform the next post that we were on our way.

'Ivan,' I asked, 'what would happen if we were to turn off to look at the landscape?'

He laughed, as if to say that no-one was supposed to stray in his country. 'The whole of the police of the Soviet Union would be searching for us within minutes.'

At Zagorsk we invited Ivan to have lunch with us and he escorted us to a restaurant along pavements slippery with ice. I thanked him as he held my arm to prevent me slipping.

'Foreign ladies understand,' he grinned, very proud of his gentlemanly behaviour. 'When I first courted my wife she told me off if I took her arm to help her, saying "What are you leaning on me for?".'

The food in the restaurant was excellent. The dishes arrived piping hot, and the helpings were liberal. Ivan was a good conversationalist, with a sense of humour, and I found myself wondering just how loyal he was to the régime. He freely admitted that Russia had a lot to learn from the West, and he didn't mean just in the realms of technology.

After lunch we strolled inside the monastery walls. My mother used to undertake a pilgrimage to Zagorsk twice a year and bring silver ikons back for us children. A few monks scurried about on the silver snow, the bright Northern light shone on the golden cupolas and for a moment I was back in the familiar, peaceful Russia of my childhood.

But there was a disappointment in store in the monastery museum. I had been informed that there were rare ikons here, but there were none on display. Ivan insisted that there was nothing else to see, but I did not believe him. I caught up with a monk who was crossing the courtyard and said 'Father, you have some rare ikons here. Where are they?'

Taken by surprise, he said 'They are in a special room,' and then he hurried away, realising that he had been indiscreet.

'I'm going back to see them!' I said defiantly to Ivan.

He didn't like it; it wasn't mentioned in the tourist guide.

'I assure you there are none,' he insisted. 'The monk is mistaken.'

'We'll soon find out,' I answered.

Helen was amused and Ivan had no choice but to follow. Back in the building I saw a door with 'Director' written on it. I barged in before anyone could stop me, followed by my companions, and before the man behind the desk had time to look surprised I said 'I understand you have a special room here full of wonderful ikons. My ambassador particularly recommended me to see them as he thought it would benefit me culturally.' (Russians love that word *kultourno*.)

'Which country's ambassador is that?' he asked.

'England's,' I answered, hoping he wouldn't call my bluff by asking the ambassador's name. 'My friends here are from X embassy.'

He glanced at them, reached for a sheet of paper, wrote something and marked it with an official stamp, and handed it to me with a gracious smile.

This permit worked wonders, as such things do in bureaucratic countries; a previously locked door was opened and we gazed at wonderful works of art displayed in three rooms for as long as we wished.

'Why aren't these ikons shown to the public?' I asked Ivan, but he couldn't offer any explanation. I often wonder what he told his masters in the KGB about our visit to Zagorsk.

We went back to the waiting car. Ivan had set the automatic heater for 3pm, as the temperature was about thirty degrees below freezing. Two young men were examining the car, obviously intrigued by its appearance and gadgets. Helen laughingly said 'Want to buy it?' in her broken Russian.

They gasped, and one of them—they couldn't have been much over twenty—said 'How could we? Where would we get enough money?' They had taken Helen quite seriously!

We got into the car, but it was so well heated that we had to open the windows a few inches. One of the young men asked politely if he could see how the various instruments worked. Helen assented, and Ivan started to explain while the other edged towards our open window. He was obviously thrilled by the idea of conversing with foreigners, of whom we were the first he had ever met.

'Please lower your window a bit more,' he begged, anxious not to miss a word of what we were saying. Because of the extreme cold we were a little unwilling, but he didn't seem to understand this, perhaps because he himself, in his fur-lined jacket, hat and enormous fur and leather gloves, was immune to any weather.

'You will come to no harm talking to me,' he said and to re-assure us he took out from his inside pocket his identity papers to prove that he was a lumberjack and had a clean record. 'Couldn't you lower the window a bit more now that you know I've never been in any trouble?' he pleaded.

I don't think he believed us when we assured him that it was the cruel Russian winter we shrank from, not from him. Suddenly, understanding flashed across his young face. 'I apologise!' he cried. 'You must forgive me. How *ne-koultorno* to speak to you with my gloves on!' and with great panache he pulled them off. After such gallantry, we were forced to grant his request and lower the window. Such childlike naïvety is one of the Russians' most charming characteristics.

The boy went on talking and asking questions; his hands went quite blue with cold but there was still a lot that he wanted to know about. 'When are you coming back to Zagorsk so that we can continue our conversation?' he asked, as Ivan started the car.

'Probably at Easter,' I said, and he waved goodbye enthusiastically. I hope he didn't wait too long that Easter; I have not been to Zagorsk since then.

Helen had been most generous in placing Ivan and her car at my disposal. He was a wonderful guide. He took me wherever I wished to go and also introduced me to parts of Moscow the existence of which I had never suspected. Helen insisted that I should not trust him, but we could not help liking him. Helen was sure that he would not have been appointed as her chauffeur if he were not an employee of the KGB, briefed to report to his masters on Helen's activities, but at the back of my mind a small doubt lingered. It was difficult to believe that he was as enthusiastic a communist as his job led us to suppose. He was inordinately interested in life in the West, and I told him everything I could about it. I answered all his questions, and asked very few in return. I never mentioned my Russian friends, pretending that all my contacts were diplomatic ones. I found him a pleasant companion, kind, attentive and helpful, and I treated him as a friend, with reservations.

Whenever any members of the diplomatic corps leave Russia the people who have served them are transferred. This is no doubt meant to prevent them from keeping in touch, because it is very rare for a Russian to tell you his address, or even his surname. During Helen's leave of absence Ivan simply disappeared, to her regret and mine.

One of the last stories he told me seemed to contain a message. His mother lived in Moscow, he said, and her brother, Ivan's uncle, came from some distant province to visit her. 'The old man had never left his village before,' Ivan explained, 'and he had never seen what our beautiful capital looks like.' So on his day off Ivan took his uncle to see the sights. He took him to the Kremlin, to the Palace of Congresses, showed him the underground and in the end they went to *Gum*, the famous department store on Red Square.

'My uncle had never seen such luxuries,' said Ivan, who was very proud of the Soviet shops. It was particularly cold and his uncle's nose was running, and as soon as they entered the sacred precincts of that store of stores he took his nose between his thumb and index finger—Russian fashion—and blew it heartily straight onto the floor among all the shoppers. Ivan was horrified that such a thing should happen to him, a 'gentleman'. 'Uncle, uncle, how can you shame me like this!' he said. 'Matushka has given you a handkerchief to use.'

'I know,' said the old man, giving his nephew a shrewd look. 'I'm keeping it to wipe my glasses with.'

'Nothing much has changed then,' I said. 'In the old days there used to be a proverb about the rich man putting in his pocket what the poor man throws away!'

Next day I had planned to do some shopping, and I managed to find a taxi to take me round the 'commission shops' where I hoped to be able to buy some antiques. The taxi-driver was a tough, cheerful-looking little man. I made myself clear: 'I want you to stick by me all morning and not drop me off in the middle of nowhere.' He agreed, took me to various 'commission shops' and enjoyed my discomfiture at not being able to buy anything. 'What do you want such rubbish for?' he asked. 'Why not buy nice new things if you've got the money?'

He was very talkative, and told me that he had fought under Joukoff and had once been to London as a staff officer. He did not approve of life in the West and found his own country much more pleasant. 'You'll soon come round to our ways,' he said. 'How soon are you going to have a communist régime in England?'

'We've already had a bloodless revolution,' I replied. 'I am the last person you should ask as I am not politically minded. All I know is that your communism deprived me of a great deal, whereas capitalism in the West has given some of it back to me.' This puzzled him and I explained at some length, concluding that I approved of a free society where one could earn one's living as one chose.

He was not convinced. 'Here everybody is equal,' he argued. 'We all work for the State, no-one grabs anything.' Our discussion became quite heated, although good-tempered. At one point he even said 'How can a nice person like you be a capitalist?'

'There is a lot of poverty and inequality in Russia,' I argued, to which he replied that the riches of the West smelt of blood and betrayals. 'In Russia no-one can be bought!'

I thought of all the tips and inducements that I had distributed, but I said nothing. I didn't want to antagonise him when he was so patiently driving me from shop to shop, by this time in search of men's handkerchiefs, which were more elusive than antiques.

In the end I gave up, and asked the taxi-driver to drive me to Helen's flat as it was nearing lunch-time. He pulled a face; it seemed that in spite of our arrangement he was unwilling to give me any more of his time. I was just dismissing the idea of giving this idealist a tip to persuade him, remembering our recent discussion, when he said 'For a really handsome tip I'll take you anywhere you like.' And he named his price. When we arrived at Helen's flat I gave him the sum we had agreed on, and he thanked me and wished me a pleasant stay in Moscow. 'Thank you,' I replied, adding, 'You must be glad I am a capitalist and able to tip you so handsomely!'

I saw Helen as often as her work would permit, and introduced her to several of my Russian friends, always in some open place such as a park, a museum or a metro station. In the Soviet Union people know that it is wise to steer clear of contact with foreign diplomats, and Helen herself was well aware of this. Sometimes I visited her in her flat, where we had many long conversations late into the night. Her flat had two rooms and a kitchen and a bathroom, which is luxurious by Soviet standards, and Helen had made it very attractive by replacing the embassy furniture with antiques bought in the 'commission shops', thus transforming it into a home where one could temporarily forget that one was in a communist country.

Helen's flat was in one of the special apartment blocks reserved for foreign diplomats and guarded day and night by sentries. She felt that her every move was watched, and that she was forced into a claustrophobic and monastic life-style that was beginning to tell on her. In fact she had become so depressed that she had asked for a transfer, and she told me a story which explained part of her depression.

At a large diplomatic reception the previous year an attractive and well-dressed man had asked her to dance. His French was flawless, and she deduced that he must be a newly appointed diplomat. They were attracted to each other and she was not surprised when he asked her out to dinner, but her heart sank when he announced that he was a Russian journalist, as any relationship between them was bound, sooner or later, to run into difficulties. However, when he escorted her home after their first date she noticed that the sentries let him pass without a query. Life became more interesting; Alexis came to see her often, they went to concerts and art galleries and spent week-ends together in the country. In fact their love-affair blossomed; Alexis anticipated her every wish; in love, to quote de Custine, 'the Russians are the gentlest wild beasts'.

And then suddenly, Alexis did not turn up as arranged one evening, and didn't telephone. He had given her a number to ring in an emergency, but when she rang an unknown voice answered. She asked to speak to Alexis, as she had done in the past; there was a slight pause, and then the voice said 'There is no-one of that name here.' She checked the number and tried again, with the same result.

A few days later her chief called her in and told her that he had received complaints about undesirable associations by his personnel with certain members of the Soviet press. He was very apologetic, and he explained that the Russians were worried about information leaking out and that, although he did not share their views, he felt obliged to warn her of their complaints. He spoke in general terms, not naming anyone, but she knew that in the confined diplomatic circles of Moscow her association with Alexis could not have been a secret, especially because of the sentries always on duty. Alexis had laughed at her fears, arguing that his government could not possibly object to a simple love affair. And now, when he had lulled her into a state of false security, it was suddenly all over.

At first she had tried to make surreptitious inquiries, but after six months she was none the wiser, and she could only hope that nothing worse had happened to Alexis than demotion or a transfer.

Helen and I sat in her flat and discussed the lack of personal freedom in Russia, and the atmosphere of fear. We personally knew of several incidents which proved how careful one has to be. A mutual friend of ours, T, was a pensioner who spent many hours in the woods, collecting strange roots and bits of wood from which he created sculptures of quite unusual artistry, representing people or animals. Helen had offered to buy some of them; he accepted and offered to deliver them when they were ready. We thought this rather risky, but presumed that he knew better. Pensioners in Russia, after all, are a rather special class. Having survived the persecutions, the prisons, the concentration camps and the war, not to speak of hunger, cold, communal living conditions and constant fear, suddenly at the age of sixty they feel liberated. The State doesn't need them any more, their movements are no longer under constant surveillance, they don't have to report for work and they have a pension which, no matter how small, gives them a sense of freedom that they have never known before. In T's case an extra factor was that he had no sons or daughters to protect.

The bell rang in Helen's flat at the appointed time. She opened the door to find T in a state of collapse, and so badly frightened that Helen thought he was going to have a heart attack. She made him sit in the nearest armchair and gave him a large dose of brandy. When he had recovered a little he explained that he had been stopped by the sentries who guarded the flats. They had searched him, examined his documents and his parcel of wooden figures, noted his name and address and also Helen's.

It was a terrifying experience because he could not know how it might end. Would they arrest him as he left? Would there be a knock on his door one night? Ever since 1917 Russians had feared this kind of thing, and Helen's reassurance did not help much. In fact as far as I know nothing has happened to T, but I am sure that he will never visit a foreigner's flat again.

Helen told me of other incidents, or 'accidents' as she preferred to call them. The house of a dissident artist she knew had been burnt down, killing him and his family, and a Russian girl secretary had died of a very unexpected heart attack at the age of thirty-five, brought on, Helen cynically suggested, by being too friendly with foreigners. On my last visit I found Helen so disillusioned, and drinking so heavily, that her recall could not be long delayed.

CHAPTER TWENTY

When I wanted to see Volodia I could only get in touch with him through Mitia, but when I approached him Mitia seemed very evasive, and I soon realised that they were not on very good terms. Apparently when I had asked Helen to assist Mitia when he was ill she had gone to Volodia's flat with some money and a parcel of clothes for Mitia. When Volodia's wife opened the door and recognised Helen as a foreigner she was quite panic-stricken, and in the end Helen gave up trying to explain that she had taken every precaution and could not have been followed, threw the parcel and the money on the table, and left. As a result Theo and Volodia had gone to see Mitia in hospital and had given him quite a lecture on the risks he was taking and the compromising position into which he was putting the whole family by having contacts with me, a dangerous foreigner, and accepting my money.

It seemed strange that my innocent act should have been so misconstrued, and I begged Mitia to let Volodia know that I was in Moscow. Soon he called me on the telephone, and apologised. He owed me an explanation, he said, and later over a lot of vodka full harmony was restored. It was then that he voiced his regret that Mitia could not be helped more in his precarious state of health, saying 'If only he could sell some of his pictures!'

This gave me an idea; I had a lot of black-market roubles left, and I decided to tell Mitia that I had friends who wanted to buy his pictures. The upshot was that he brought a lot of his paintings to my room. At that stage I hadn't given much thought to the problem of getting them out of the country.

Meanwhile I had promised Helen some tickets for *Spartacus* at the Bolshoi Theatre. I had made friends with Nina Petrovna in the ticket office, but when I approached her she said she was sorry but she couldn't let me have a single ticket. But she did tell me which ticket office had been given the largest allocation, and I was at the head of the queue when it opened.

'Can I buy theatre tickets here for dollars?' I asked.

The reply was evasive. 'It all depends on what you want to see.'

The girl with the tickets had not yet arrived, so I decided to wait. The girls in the office chatted among themselves, little expecting that any foreigner would be able to understand them. Suddenly one of them mentioned that 'Elena' was on her way with quite a few tickets for the ballet I wanted to see. I started digging in my black bag for bait, and by the time Elena arrived the girls and I were on the best of terms. I moved away to give them a chance to brief her. When I returned five minutes later she smiled and said 'I understand you would like tickets for *Spartacus*. You know you have to pay in dollars?'

I plunged my hand into my bag for stockings and perfume.

'How many tickets would you like ?' Elena asked. 'Would you like stalls, or perhaps a box . . .?'

'Could I have Beignoir Box eight, left side?' I asked. Elena seemed surprised at so precise a request. 'It used to be my family's box where I was taken as a child once a week,' I explained. 'Capitalistic privileges of days gone by,' I added, as Elena and her companions gasped.

And so it came about that I watched the performance of *Spartacus* with Helen and her friends from the very box where I had sat with my parents as a little girl.

'You are luckier than our ambassador,' said Helen. 'When he applies for seats like these his application always gets refused.'

Helen's friends thought me omnipotent. 'It's marvellous,' they said, 'how quickly you have learnt the intricacies of Soviet life. Knowing the language must be a great help. You don't by any chance know where we could buy paintings by a modern Russian artist?'

I could hardly believe my ears. I invited them round to my hotel room after the performance. 'How many can we buy?' they asked when they saw the paintings.

'You can have the lot,' I said, 'on one condition. Pay me now and in roubles. The price I leave to your generosity; the artist is poor and you are his only clients.'

They were very generous and I slept with a large wad of notes under my pillow. Next morning I was so excited that I could hardly wait to telephone Mitia.

'Have you any more paintings?' I asked.

'Yes, of course; don't you like the ones you have already?'
'I don't know. I haven't made up my mind.'
He arrived shortly afterwards, looking slightly dejected. 'You mean you don't like any of the paintings I brought you?'
I silently shook my head and made a gesture to indicate that all the paintings had vanished, and at the same time handed him a wad of notes. I helped him to stuff the money into his pockets and in the anonymous safety of the street I explained what had happened. He was like a man who had won a large sum on the football pools. He started building castles in Spain, and I had to bring him down to earth and recommend discretion. 'Keep the money under your mattress and spend a little of it at a time,' I advised.

We celebrated by going with Olga to a performance at the Palace of Congresses. The enormous auditorium with 6,000 seats was quite awe-inspiring but I couldn't help wondering what would happen if there was a fire.

The coat I was wearing had a sable lining which had seen better days, but Olga had spotted it and begged me to let her wear it. In the interval she paraded in it and returned starry-eyed to confide that everyone had stared at her because of the beautiful fur. I found this complete lack of sophistication most endearing.

After the performance we went to see a young couple, friends of Olga, who were ardent balletomanes. Ever since my first visit I had been sending them periodicals describing ballet performances all around the world. When we met that evening I discovered that they hadn't received all of them, and we worked out that the ones that hadn't got through had all had references to the two defectors, Nureyev and Makarova. Evidently the Russian government censors all references to citizens who have the effrontery to choose a different life.

Our hosts switched on the television to see the latest news. The shooting of a fourteen-year-old boy in Belfast was very unflatteringly reported. My friends joined in the condemnation of it and were quite justly incensed. 'What is the British Army going to do next?' they asked. 'Fancy shooting a boy of fourteen!' I think they expected a heated argument to follow, but I put a stop to that by saying 'If you want to develop this particular subject further, why not discuss the Russian Army's invasions of Hungary and Czechoslovakia first?'

At breakfast the next morning the café was half empty. An English girl who had come to Russia on the same flight as I joined me at my table. We were just discussing our various visits to Russian theatres when a colossus of a man entered the café. He must have been nearly seven feet tall; he wore a beard, had a splendid physique and looked the incarnation of the typical Russian *boyar*. He sat down, surveyed the room, looked inquiringly at the ceiling and in a thundering voice demanded service. He wanted everything on the menu and several things which weren't, and he wanted it double quick—especially the drink, of which he appeared already to have had plenty. Soon all the waitresses were lending a hand, intrigued by this good-looking giant of about thirty-five snapping orders at them. Soon there was a fine array of bottles in front of him, vodka, madeira, champagne, which he arranged in rows before gulping large quantities of each quite indiscriminately and then bellowing for more. I watched over the English girl's shoulder, astonished and amused by this stranger's capacity to eat and drink. He must have seen me watching, for he suddenly gave a broad grin in my direction, reached for the champagne bottle and, lifting his glass, roared across the room 'To you, Madam!'

I ducked behind the English girl but he was not to be discouraged. He leaned sideways and lifted his glass again. For some reason drunks have always been attracted to me! I went on with my breakfast, pretending not to notice, and the man went on toasting me.

All at once, with a terrific racket, he pushed away his chair, rose unsteadily to his feet, gathered a couple of bottles under each arm, picked up two glasses and marched towards our table. Next moment he was towering over me, clicking his heels and bowing as he introduced himself. 'We do not speak Russian,' I said, pointing to my companion. He glanced at her, looked me straight in the eyes and repeated his name. He put a glass on the table in front of me, drew up a chair, put his bottles on the table and poured out two glasses of champagne.

'You cannot fool me, I know you must speak Russian,' he said softly. Not prepared to argue with a drunk I spoke to him severely: 'You should not accost people like that. We are foreigners and my white hair should command your respect.'

'What has age to do with it?' he retorted. 'I have not seen or talked to a civilised being for over fifteen years.' He grabbed my hand and kissed it.

The English girl looked on in great surprise, and all the waitresses watched as the stranger once more raised his glass and begged me to drink with him. 'I cannot, I have scarcely finished my breakfast,' I protested. 'But you must. Where I come from, if you don't drink with a man it means that you despise him. You don't despise me?' he asked, almost in a whisper. There was something akin to fear in his voice, and such urgency that I had to relent. Besides, I thought it might pacify him. So, raising my glass, I sipped it and said 'I drink your health!'

I had not anticipated his reaction. He jumped to his feet as if he had been stung, raised himself to his full height—a fine figure of a man—and laughed bitterly.

'No, you don't have to drink to that,' he cried. 'Look at me! Why do you think I have survived?' And he sat down and refilled his glass.

The English girl decided to leave. I rose too; Mitia was waiting for me. But the stranger touched my shoulder and resolutely pressed me down again. '*Matushka*,' (little mother) he pleaded, his eyes as gentle and persuasive as those of a child, 'please stay a little longer. We shall never see each other again so let's talk for a few more minutes; let's drink to my future—for I shall have one!' he asserted defiantly.

Suddenly it dawned on me. 'Where do you come from?' I asked, almost certain what the answer would be.

'I have come from Kolyma,' he answered. 'Do you know where that is?'

The name is linked with Russia's worst concentration camps. In my mind I started counting the years. This was 1972, and he had been away for fifteen years, which took us back to 1957. Stalin had died in 1953, so he had not been condemned under the Stalinist purges. Suddenly I needed no persuasion. I was eager to learn his story.

He had been arrested as an unruly student of twenty. He had been living with his mother—his father had been shot during Stalin's reign and he had been marked down as a result. He considered that he had been given a light sentence, ten plus five, which meant ten years' hard labour followed by five years' exile. He had returned to Moscow that very morning and he was leaving shortly. He did not reveal his destination, nor did he mention his mother's fate. His story was very incoherent; he was quite drunk by this time. Nevertheless, the salient facts were quite clear. For fifteen years he had been cut off from the world and lived under circumstances that people used to freedom can scarcely imagine. But there was no bitterness in him. He was not crying over his broken life. He even considered that prison had saved him from youthful aberrations and that it had been spiritually beneficial. For years he had lived from day to day, not knowing in the morning whether he would be alive by nightfall. He had come to appreciate life and he rejoiced that he had won the battle for survival in the concentration camps. He was determined to win yet another battle, by re-establishing himself and building a new life in the world from which he had been an outcast.

I didn't ask what his crime had been; so many men in the Soviet Union have been in prison at some time in their lives. Now, as in the twenties, one still asks 'Did you sit?', which means 'Have you been in prison?' I didn't do much talking at all. The man had to unburden himself, and for some reason he had chosen me. Perhaps I reminded him of his mother. He talked quietly and confidentially, calling me '*Matushka*' (little mother) until Tania, who was obviously worried and had been making signs to me all the while, came up to the table.

'Comrade, it's time you went. You'll get yourself back where you came from if you go on talking to foreigners.' He did not answer. He paid his bill from an enormous wad of notes, kissed both my hands, said 'Bless me, *Matushka*, and wish me luck,' and was gone.

I stared at Tania. 'Where did all that money come from?' I asked.

'They all come back loaded—those that come back,' she said. 'The last years when they're in exile they work in the mines. The pay is good and there's nothing to spend it on, and when they come back they usually have a big bank-roll with them.'

'Have you ever met a man from Kolyma before?' I asked.

'Not that I know of. That one was nice, I wish there were more like him! That's why I didn't want any trouble. He's suffered enough. Some of our men are such pigs.'

Her last sentence surprised me. 'How do you mean?'

'Well, they treat me like dirt just because I'm a waitress.'

'I thought that everyone in your country was equal?'

'You can't think that,' she said. 'You must have noticed how people in authority treat their subordinates. When I was at university I went steady with a lieutenant, but his commanding officer soon put a stop to it when I took this job. Now I'm only good enough for a factory worker or another waiter. D'you call that equality?'

CHAPTER TWENTY-ONE

The next time I went to Russia I went with my sister to see the May Day celebrations in Moscow. At Intourist in London I booked what was described as 'Moscow Stars Theatre Festival'. We were to fly to Leningrad on 29 April and, after a night in a hotel and a sightseeing tour of the city, we were to be flown to Moscow for May Day.

When we had arrived at Leningrad and had gone through the usual formalities I asked for a taxi, as I had always done on earlier visits, only to be told that we were to be taken to our hotel by bus. An old man, who was recovering from a stroke and travelling with a young companion, also complained that he had paid for such amenities as taxis. As usual, the Intourist girl assured us that it would all be sorted out when we arrived at our hotel. But instead of the promised Leningrad Hotel, the bus took us in the opposite direction, to the Sovietskaya Hotel, and as soon as we arrived the guide announced that we were to assemble in the hall in one hour's time to be driven to the Astoria for dinner.

'Why can't we have dinner here?' I protested. 'We are all tired and the Astoria is a half-hour journey away.'

'Sorry, arrangements have already been made,' said the guide laconically.

At the Astoria all fifty-two of us sat down at one table, where we had to eat what was put before us—there was no *à la carte*, no caviar, and we were polished off in no time.

'Tomorrow I will collect vouchers so that we can lunch and dine where and when we please,' I said to my sister Tousia. But after dinner there was a further announcement. Would all tourists please be ready by half past nine next morning to be taken by bus to the Astoria for breakfast? This was too much. I demanded food vouchers such as we had always been given previously. 'We do not issue any, everything is taken care of for you,' was the firm reply.

'I'm sorry,' I said, 'but we do not choose to be like a lot of sheep.'

'There are no vouchers,' she repeated.

'In that case we will have to spend foreign currency. We simply refuse to be dragged miles for breakfast.'

I was furious. So was the Intourist girl. We glared at each other, while the other tourists looked on and wondered what the argument was all about.

Next morning we breakfasted at the hotel; many of our fellow tourists said that they would have liked to do the same, had it not been for the language barrier. The guide sought me out. 'Will you at least join us for lunch? It has been ordered for you.'

'No thank you. We have made other arrangements.'

She was annoyed, but there was little she could do. 'We're leaving for Moscow this evening, so will you all please vacate your rooms by noon,' she announced.

'What time is the plane?' I asked.

'We are going by train at eleven.'

'But we were supposed to fly to Moscow?'

'I'm sorry,' she said, 'but we are going by train.'

'What are we supposed to do until eleven?'

'A special rest-room will be provided.'

I grumbled that this was not what we had expected when we had paid for first-class accommodation, and the excursion bus that morning went off without us. Two men from the group chose to 'go native' with us, and we took a tram into the centre of the town. There are no conductors on Russian public transport; you are trusted to pay your fare by putting your kopeks into a box provided for the purpose, which most people scrupulously do, although I saw a sticker on one Moscow tram which gave the name and address of a woman who had not done so, and was thus exposed to her fellow travellers.

Walking towards the Admiralty we bought ice-creams—the best in the world—and discussed the inefficiency of the Intourist organisation. Presently a young man came up to us and in quite good English started praising the beauties of Leningrad. We tried to shake him off, and finally he said 'Can't you sell me something?' We assured him that we had nothing to sell, and he walked off in disgust.

We left our companions at the Astoria and hailed a taxi to

take us back to our hotel, where we found the restaurant full of German tourists. A waitress tried to turn us away. 'Surely we can have lunch? We have been well treated here before,' I said, and offered her some chewing-gum.

'All right,' she said, 'if you are not too difficult to please.'

She brought us our order—there was little choice on the menu, and no caviar again—and then she went to join one of the other waitresses and beckoned to a third. Obviously something was brewing. Presently two of them came up to us and asked us if we were satisfied. We got into conversation—they told us that their names were Tania and Zina—and when they left the third girl came up and sat down with customary familiarity at our table. Without preamble she said 'Can you do something for us? There are folding umbrellas at the *beriozka* shop for five dollars each. Could you buy two if I gave you ten dollars?'

When I consented she said she would have to telephone someone to bring the foreign currency. 'Don't worry,' I said, 'we'll buy the umbrellas and come back here for dinner. You can settle up then.'

The *beriozka* shops are for foreign tourists, and I noted that vodka was very cheap, although Russians had complained bitterly to us at the high price they had to pay for vodka. We bought the umbrellas and found the rest room at the hotel, where we had to sit among the cases of the other fifty members of our tour. But it was better to sit among the luggage than to tramp the streets. At six o'clock we went back into the restaurant, where the waitresses spotted us at once. We were very courteously received; the menu was brought with a ten-dollar bill inside it, and we deposited the umbrellas underneath our table. Tania and Zina brought us a plate covered with a white napkin on which lay two bars of chocolate—a charming gesture which reminded us of the old semitic custom of offering bread and salt. This was followed by smoked fish, which they regarded as a great delicacy, although we did not enjoy it much. We dined quietly, lingering until ten o'clock, and when we asked for our bill we were told that our meal had been paid for by the three girls who, having finished their spell of duty and collected their umbrellas, had gone home.

Our group had already assembled in the hall. The weather had changed, and it was raining as we boarded the bus; by the time we reached the station it was a real downpour, and as the station platform was not covered we were all soaked to the skin by the time we reached our train. We scrambled in with our hand luggage and found a compartment with two suitable companions, an Australian woman and a girl librarian. We hung our wet clothes to dry on the rail in the corridor outside, and soon everyone else followed suit until it looked like a bargain basement on sale day, with trousers, dresses and jackets hanging on the rail and pairs of shoes hung up on strings.

Our heavier luggage was being looked after by Intourist, so we assumed that it would be put in the guard's van. Such assumptions are unwise in the Soviet Union, and the heavy and wet cases were thrown indiscriminately into the corridor of the train, adding to the existing chaos and making it almost impossible to pass. Passengers searching for their luggage to make sure that it hadn't been lost didn't help matters, and at that moment the attendant came down the corridor distributing sheets and blankets. An elderly person asked her if she could please make up her berth. 'Do it youself,' she replied.

The train was very stuffy and it proved impossible to open the windows. There was only one toilet for the fifty-two tourists, and we soon saw that our travelling companions were very disenchanted with travel in Russia by this time. The Australian girl bought herself a cup of tea which she put on the small plastic table. The attendant spotted it, muttered '*Ne koultourno!*' and grumpily put a towel underneath the cup. We removed the towel, assuring her that our behaviour was perfectly *koultourno*. By now we were in complete revolt and were mentally composing letters of complaint to all and sundry.

Sleep was impossible. The stuffiness and the smell of wet clothes saw to that. The train crawled, stopping continually, and the water in the loo ran out; we just had to hope that we could last out to the end of the journey. The attendant vanished, leaving us locked in the train, in spite of the notice which informed her of her duties to her passengers. The whole journey was a nightmare.

The train pulled in to Moscow station at nine in the morning, after a nine-hour journey. We were worn out by our sleepless night, but I tried to cheer my sister up by repeating the brochure's glowing description of the new Intourist hotel in Red Square, where we should be able to see the May Day celebrations in comfort from our room.

A new guide introduced herself and shepherded us into a bus. Through her loudspeaker she announced that we were going to the Leningradsky Hotel, next to the station. Our group had, up till now, been a fairly good-humoured and patient lot in spite of everything—most of the complaints had come from me. But now, as the guide finished speaking, they started to voice their annoyance. 'Why aren't you taking us to the Intourist hotel in Red Square?' 'We want to see the May Day celebrations; that was why we came!' 'The Leningradsky's nowhere near the centre; how are we going to travel into town?'

The guide was unperturbed. 'The centre of the city is already closed to the public anyway,' she said.

'How are we supposed to see the celebrations?' asked an angry Scotsman.

'You can see them on television in your hotel rooms.'

At that the tourists really got indignant, and started demanding to see someone in authority. I was delighted. 'About time,' I thought. 'Maybe now we'll get something done.'

The Scotsman said 'I'm going to Red Square with my friend. Do you want to come?'

'We are far too tired,' I said, 'but good luck all the same.'

'Don't mention it to the guide,' he said. 'Let her look for us!'

The hotel was spacious and comfortable, and a hot bath did something to revive us. We were badly in need of sleep, but I telephoned Nastia to get rid of at least one suitcase as soon as possible. The less we had in our hotel room the better, as it was almost certain to be inspected as soon as we went out. I told Nastia the name of our hotel and our room number, and she knocked on our door about an hour later. She was very upset; just as she had been about to enter the lift she had been stopped, told to produce her identity papers and asked whom she was about to visit. In her panic she forgot my surname, but she had given my room number and they had let her pass. The experience had unnerved her and she was too afraid to carry the suitcase out of the hotel. Leaving Tousia to get some rest, I carried the bag myself, saying in a loud voice 'I must first call at my embassy to deposit the bag' as I went past the spy-girl on our floor. We went to Nastia's flat by the comparatively anonymous underground.

Over a meal, which I very much enjoyed, I told Nastia about

the discomforts of our trip and she crossed herself and sighed, a typically Russian reaction which gave me small comfort. I also asked her if she had seen anything of Tania.

Nastia was apparently very bitter about her. She had gone to see her at the café but had found no sign of her, and her inquiries were fruitless. No-one gives any information away in the Soviet Union. She returned again and again until one day the doorman let slip that Tania had been promoted and was in charge of food supplies on the floor above. Nastia had gone up, taking the latest parcel of clothes that I had sent for Tania, and had found her queening it among fruit, caviar and all manner of almost unobtainable provisions. 'She never even offered me an apple,' Nastia complained, 'and the price of caviar has trebled.'

I too was disappointed in Tania, but I knew that life for her had not exactly been a bed of roses. I took some food back for Tousia and hurried to the hotel to catch up on some sleep.

Next morning I discovered another innovation. We could have breakfast in our rooms! I telephoned for room service as instructed in the pamphlet, and within ten minutes we were brought tea, bread, butter, jam and a bottle of *kefir*. Then I went down to the hall so that I could meet Mitia without him being asked to produce his identity papers. Seeing the Scotsman and anxious to find out how he had got on in the May Day parade, I went over to him.

'You missed the fun,' he said. 'My friend and I were arrested by the KGB. Very neatly done it was too!'

It turned out that he was an evangelist and had come to Russia expressly to distribute Bibles. The previous morning he and his friend had had a rendezvous with other evangelists but they had missed it because of the train journey. As they watched the parade, they could not resist the temptation to intone 'Onward Christian soldiers'. Very smartly two military policemen hemmed them in and next thing they knew they were being interviewed by the KGB. 'They kept us there for hours and we had quite a conversation,' he said, 'but for every question they asked, I asked one back! A Russian in the corner of the room was scared out of his wits, but when we were brought in we insisted on shaking hands with the guards. I must say it surprised them!'

'I hope you didn't take that opportunity to preach the Scriptures,' I said.

'No,' he laughed, 'but I kept asking whether Lenin really was in the mausoleum.'

'Why did you do that?'

'So that I could tell them that when Jesus Christ's tomb was opened He was not there! I think they got so fed up with us they were only too anxious to let us go, but they had to wait until the May Day parade was over. They've put a tail on me, he's over there,' and he pointed to a nondescript individual lurking in the foyer.

His distribution of Bibles was severely hampered because he was unable to buy a plan of Moscow, so I gave him mine. He said he would get it reproduced when he got back to England. I already knew about the activities of such evangelists in Russia, but we had never met one before. Both Tousia and I were impressed by his zeal and courage.

'Do you think our train was delayed because the authorities had some suspicion that you had infiltrated our group?' I asked him.

'What makes you ask that?'

'A Russian friend of mine who listens to the BBC told me that he had heard a few days ago that some evangelists were coming to Moscow for the May Day celebrations, and you know how edgy the authorities here are about that sort of thing.'

At this point we were interrupted by Mitia's arrival. His reunion with Tousia was very emotional. They had parted young and on the threshold of life, and now, meeting fifty years later, they were a couple of old folk. Because they wanted to swap memories, we took a train to a nearby place out in the country so that they could talk freely.

It is at first very strange always to go into a public place or into the open country in order to be able to exchange ideas, but it explained past references in letters from Russia to what seemed a disproportionate amount of time spent mushrooming in summer and skiing in winter. When you live as confined as most Russian city dwellers, with neighbours you cannot trust and scarcely enough space to store essentials, it is quite natural to want to escape into nature's freedom.

Volodia's escape was his allotment, which supplied all kinds of home-made fare. Every time a certain kind of produce was mentioned he was liable to reach under one of the divan beds where he stacked jars of such things. In spite of his poverty, his hospitality was princely.

On one occasion I refused some egg mayonnaise. He was quite annoyed, saying 'To think I stood in a queue for six hours because I thought you would enjoy it!'

'Volodia, how awful!' I gasped.

'Well, it's simply a case of bad distribution. When I arrived home my wife told me that there were plenty available at our next-door dairy!'

'What a waste of time,' I remarked.

'How do you do your shopping in London?' he asked.

'I whizz round in my little Mini, and in fifteen minutes it's all over,' I said.

Everyone present smiled, but nothing was said and we carried on with some other topic of conversation. Suddenly Volodia interrupted:

'What if there are a lot of people in the shop? A long queue? What do you do then?'

'I simply pop into another shop,' I said. There was an outburst of laughter. 'What have I said that's so funny?' I asked.

'Well, it's the way you exaggerate,' Volodia explained.

It was my turn to laugh. It was no use explaining that in England shops were next door to each other, while in Russia they are miles apart. They would not have believed me.

Nevertheless, on this visit I did notice a considerable improvement in Russian shops, although there were still always queues for fruit and fresh vegetables. Life for the ordinary man in the street had definitely become easier during the years in which I had been visiting Russia; unfortunately, their treatment of tourists had become much worse!

We spent most of our days visiting places off the beaten track, places with no tourist attractions, and often out of bounds. It was risky, but it was well worth it. We had endless talks with all manner of ordinary Russian people, who were cautious and guarded until we gained their confidence and drew them out. Sometimes we wondered if we were really in a communist country, because as soon as we got away from Intourist we met very few people who seemed to be true communists. One taxi driver told me that there were actually only about a million communists in the whole Soviet Union.

'If there are so few,' I asked, 'how do you explain the endless queue to visit Lenin's tomb?'

'People who work in factories and offices have to go there.'

'What do you mean, "have to"?'

'Well, it's all part of the job. When the authorities tell us to visit the tomb, it's healtheir not to argue. On public holidays they even provide us with flowers,' he added sarcastically.

'So all this veneration of Lenin is forced upon people by the State? Is that what you are saying?'

He nodded.

In the comparative freedom which our trips into the country afforded, I mentioned some of the things that were troubling me to a friend of Olga who had been a fairly high-ranking officer under Stalin. He was now retired and a widower, and he wanted to marry an ageing actress who accepted his adulation and allowed him to take her dog for walks but refused to accept any other advances. Olga resented this treatment of her friend and urged him to look elsewhere. There was something very pathetic in the way these ageing people discussed the problems that belong to youth.

This army officer felt very deeply about the way Kruschev had been treated. 'After all, he gave eight million people their good names back'—he was referring to the rehabilitation of men liberated from Stalin's camps—'and we didn't even give him a state funeral.'

'What is your explanation of it?'

'There is still a hard core of Stalinists,' he replied. 'Although they are a minority, they are very active, like many minorities, and they crush all opposition even now.'

'How do you all stand for it?' I asked. 'It's incomprehensible.'

'I suppose we have always loved the knout, and whoever wields it, wins,' he answered sadly.

His uncle, a victim of Stalin's purges, had died in a concentration camp. His aunt, old and broken in spirit, was left without a pension. 'I had to keep her, otherwise she would have starved. At that time I was due for promotion. The KGB summoned me instead. "You are lucky we have not arrested you for helping an enemy of the people," they said. I never got my promotion, but when my uncle's name was cleared in Kruschev's time the same KGB official came to congratulate me. That is Soviet justice for you!'

Olga had spent her holidays the previous year on a *poutevka* (a free travel voucher with a certain number of days on full board) at one of the many rest houses in the Soviet Union, most of which are old private mansions. She wanted us to see it, and as it was on the Moskva river we took a boat at one of the river stations. The Moskva, like most Russian rivers, is tremendously wide and the improvements on it since the days of my youth have been very extensive. Along its whole length it is continually intercepted by canals connecting it to other waterways all the way to the Volga river system. The sight of this expanse of lovely, clear, limpid water flowing peacefully by is most enjoyable, and the ramifications of the waterway system are most impressive.

'Yes,' agreed our friends, as I enthused. 'But it was dearly paid for. We say that it is built on human bones, because of all the forced labour gangs who perished here in their millions digging these waterways.'

God knows how many longings, desires, temptations and sufferings were buried here. And yet here was Olga pointing out the beauty spots, so pleased with life and with her country. 'You should come back and settle here,' she said. 'Life is so good now.' How quickly people forgot! And yet Olga's life was in no way enviable. She lived with her mother, who was ninety, in a one-room flat. The old lady's mind wandered and she was incontinent. She had a bed in the corner of the tiny kitchen which she left only to go to the loo. Olga occupied the other room. She was a widow, and her son was a hopeless drunkard; her friend Mitia was as poor as she was, although he was a real handyman who could even alter her dresses.

Her apartment was in a fairly new block on the site of an old village on the southern outskirts of the town. The old village had been demolished and the previous inhabitants intermixed with city dwellers, factory workers, intellectuals and whoever else had been allotted living space there. This mixed population had little in common; they distrusted each other, so there was little contact between them. From Olga's window I watched former peasants who had lost their land rummaging about on small plots or allotments surrounding the compound. And if the peasants suffered from no longer having their land, the city dwellers complained because they were too far from the centre and hated living among peasants.

An old professor and his beautiful daughter lived on Olga's landing. The girl had large, extraordinarily beautiful eyes; she was so striking that when we went with her to the theatre people turned round to stare at her. She was twenty-four and not married; their friends remarked on this. Her father said 'They criticise my daughter for being single, but who is there for her to marry? Here there are only *moujiks* who come home drunk every Saturday night and beat their wives, an old Russian custom that communism has not been able to stamp out. There's no-one left good enough for her to marry!'

Olga preferred to look on the bright side. She was happy to be sixty and a pensioner. 'In Stalin's time,' she told me, 'I was once late for work. I was petrified. I could have been sent to prison for less. Now, at last, I am no longer afraid.' Like most of her compatriots, she loved theatres and concerts, was mad on sport, swam and played volleyball. She even tried to persuade me to go to a Soviet hairdresser.

'Whatever for?' I asked.

'To have your hair dyed. Then you could remarry.'

'But I don't want to get married.'

She couldn't understand that. 'I have a friend of seventy-eight,' she told me, 'who plays volleyball twice a week and has just married a man of the same age.' She then explained that this meant that the couple would be allocated more living-space and a better pension, which made it a little more understandable.

Tousia was keen to visit the factory that our family had once owned, and to see our former home; I wanted to take some photographs. So we hired a car and directed the driver to the familiar gates and rang the bell of the janitor's lodge. A tough-looking man half opened the door and immediately closed it again, but a few seconds later a very old woman appeared and asked us what we wanted.

'We are the granddaughters of the man who founded the Red Rose a hundred years ago, and we have come to visit it,' I said. What happened then was most extraordinary. The old woman's face was transfigured, her eyes filled with tears and she crossed herself in the old Russian way.

'To think I have lived to see this moment!' she cried. 'Which of the three brothers was your father? I came to work for them in 1914. I knew them well; they were good men.'

'We are Andrew's daughters.'

'How is he?' she wanted to know.

'He's long been dead; all of them are,' I answered, and again she crossed herself.

We talked almost like old friends. She asked about the family and gave us news of old retainers. She was happy, she said, that God had allowed her to see us once more before she died. 'Today the factory is closed, but come back on Monday and we will show you everything,' she assured us, while the man who had first opened the door watched silently, nodding his head.

We were jubilant. It was a real homecoming; although strong forces had been at work, here was someone who still remembered. It had all seemed so easy; looking forward to Monday, we were driven away past what had been our family's property, and past Tolstoy's house (now a museum) in the garden of which I had often played as a little girl. We saw the little jewel of a church where Tolstoy was married, and which has now been restored to its former splendour. It had been the gift of the textile manufacturers of Moscow, and had been built on our land. Then we continued to the Novodivitchy Monastery, where we used to go with our nanny at Easter. We walked in the cemetery, reading inscriptions on the tombstones. Kruschev had been laid to rest here; we found his grave, and also that of Stalin's wife Alleluieva. There were fresh flowers on both graves.

On the Monday we arranged for a taxi to take us to the Red Rose; on the way there we bought a large box of chocolates for the old woman we had met the previous Saturday. We rang the bell, and a different woman opened the door.

'We were here on Saturday and were told to come back today,' I explained.

'What for?' she asked.

I told her who we were, adding 'My sister would like to see the house where she was born'—surely an innocuous enough request. At that moment the old lady we had seen on Saturday walked past. She pretended never to have seen us; turning her back, she began to sort out something or other. There was no question of giving her the chocolates; we could only play her game and not recognise her. We guessed that she had been severely ticked off for her friendliness to us.

'This is a working day,' the woman said. 'It is impossible to take anyone off the production line just to satisfy your frivolous request.'

'I'm not asking you to take anyone off the production line,' I said. 'Surely we could at least just have a peep at the house through the gate there?'

'It is forbidden,' the woman answered sternly.

I persisted. It was too ridiculous to be true. 'Can't you ring someone in authority, the manager or whoever is in charge?'

'I cannot do it. You will have to ask yourself on the telephone outside.'

Leaving Tousia in the lodge, I went to the telephone booth outside the gates. Finally I was put through to a woman who, after a lot of persuasion, consented to see us. When she came she was icy and unsmiling, and said that she could do nothing without a permit from the Ministry of the Interior.

'Can't you even open the door into the courtyard so that we can look at the house from there?' I asked her.

The answer was no. 'Anyway,' she went on, 'you were here two years ago and we showed it to you then. So why do you want to disrupt everything again?'

'I didn't disrupt anything then nor do I wish to do so now,' I protested. 'Surely it is natural for my sister to want to see it? This is the first time she has been in Russia for over fifty years.'

'Then you must obtain a permit from the Ministry.'

The Ministry was about ten kilometres away, but by then I had got the bit between my teeth. We reached the Ministry still clasping the large box of chocolates, and entered a large hall full of women in kerchiefs, talking, answering the telephones, cleaning floors, sorting letters. It looked more like a bazaar. We chose a kind-looking woman, made a little speech and offered her some chocolates for her grandchildren, and asked to see someone in authority.

Presently a young secretary escorted us to a second-floor office. We were interviewed by a very attractive, very gracious woman of about forty-five. I went over the whole family history and the founding of the factory by my grandfather 100 years ago,

216

and I explained our wish to revisit the place where we had spent our childhood. She listened very sympathetically.

'Perhaps you would also like to visit the factory?' she asked. 'We are very proud of the Red Rose; it is something of a show-place. I am ashamed to admit that I myself have never been inside it, so perhaps I could come with you?'

This was a real breakthrough. I had not expected it to be so easy. She sent her secretary to the Minister, asking her to explain the situation fully, and we carried on chatting. Time passed and the secretary did not return. I was worried about an appointment I had with Lera, whom I had at last managed to trace. Eventually I left before the secretary returned, but not before Comrade Taigina (she had by now told us her name) assured us that everything would be alright and that we would meet in two days' time to visit both the house and the factory together. I thanked her profusely; from now on, I felt sure, everything would run smoothly.

When I got back to the hotel I began to wonder how I should recognise Lera. It had not been easy to trace her. I had heard nothing from her until 1953, when I received a letter addressed to Nice in my maiden name. She was married, she said, and had a son and a daughter; and she would like me to write to her. I replied, but heard no more from her until 1965, when she wrote to me in London, asked for news, and failed to reply to my letter.

In the Soviet Union there are no telephone directories, but it is possible to inquire at special inquiry offices, giving the name and last known address of anyone you wish to trace. Eventually Mitia had traced her to a small derelict house, found her not at home, and left a note saying that I was in Moscow. She did not reply to this note until a fortnight before my *next* trip to Russia, and although I immediately let her know my hotel room number, I was quite surprised when she telephoned the next morning. Her voice sounded young and excited. 'To think that we will meet again after fifty years! You promised you would return!' She seemed overjoyed.

By three o'clock, tired of waiting for her, I wrote her a note to say how disappointed I had been. Could she ring and arrange another time?

A month after I had returned to London she wrote to say how

sorry she was that we had not met. 'You should come and see me. I have such a nice flat now, with a telephone. You can ring me from London any evening you like after seven o'clock.' But I never did.

We had tried to contact another childhood friend who lived in an old part of Moscow. We entered the dirty courtyard of an old apartment building and asked the women sitting gossiping if they knew where our friend lived. Following their directions we climbed a filthy stone staircase and went along a corridor where there were communal washing and cooking facilities. It was very sordid and depressing, and there was no answer to our knock. We left a note, giving only our Christian names and Mitia's telephone number, but there was no reply. We drew our own conclusions, guessing that she did not dare to contact us, and so we did not persist; but we were saddened to think of a woman who had once been a close friend eking out a miserable existence in such a dingy place.

Tousia had stayed behind with Comrade Taigina in case the permit came through for our visit to the Red Rose. When she got back to the hotel she was grinning like a Cheshire cat. She waved a scrap of paper at me. 'Taigina has arranged everything. She is going to meet us at 10am on Thursday and we are going there together. You are to explain what has happened at the Intourist office and ask them to telephone the Minister, Mr Sorokine, who knows all about it. This is his telephone number.'

I rushed to the office. A particularly obliging girl was at the desk; she looked surprised but did what I asked, and when she asked for the Minister she was curtly informed that any such request should be made in writing. As we were leaving on the following Friday, this was out of the question. I was furious by now. I dialled the Ministry and asked for Comrade Taigina's extension. She already knew what had happened. 'You don't know how sorry and upset we all are,' she said. 'We simply cannot understand it. There must be something at the factory which they don't want you to see.'

'Don't give me that,' I interrupted. 'I confided in you and talked to you like a civilised person, but I should have known better. Fifty years after the revolution the red tape, stupidity and prejudice are worse than in any capitalist country!'

'I beg you,' she pleaded, 'don't feel like that. If you like I will

218

go personally to the Minister and ask him to revoke his decision?'

Maybe she was sincere, but I no longer believed any of them. 'Don't bother,' I replied. 'But I would like you to give him a message from me.'

'Certainly,' she replied.

'Tell him to go to Hell.' And I hung up.

When I went back to our room I found that Mitia (who had just arrived) and Tousia were in a state of great agitation.

'There has just been a telephone call from the administrator of the hotel asking Mitia to report there,' said Tousia. This sounded ominous and we all three knew it; Mitia was nervous and had gone very pale.

'I'm coming with you,' I said. Downstairs the administrator was waiting.

'You asked to see me,' Mitia began.

'And I want to know why,' I interrupted, my tone deliberately angry and provoking. She looked at me condescendingly.

'No-one is allowed to go up to a guest's room without our permission,' she said.

'I will do as I please,' I retorted. 'If I wish to have twenty people in my room, that's my business.'

The administrator looked surprised but not put off. 'You should read the conditions printed on the tag of your key,' she said. 'Besides, when you are in a strange monastery you must abide by its rules.'

'I didn't bother to read your stupid rules,' I said. 'And I'm not in a strange monastery, I am your honoured guest. It is you who want tourists to come here, because you need foreign currency.'

I grabbed Mitia's arm, whispering 'Get out quickly, and don't come back.' I glared at the woman and, shaking with rage, rushed back to our room. On the way I passed the floor-spy at her desk, and remembered how I had heard her report a visitor, inquiring whether he had the necessary permission. Suddenly I knew it was her who had informed on us. Marching towards her desk, I started talking loudly to myself in Russian, cursing the régime, the red tape, the prejudice and the deplorable habit of spying on tourists. She couldn't help hearing me.

'Are you talking to yourself?' she asked.

'Yes,' I said. 'I take it that this is not forbidden to foreigners

in your country? Would you like me to repeat it all to you?'
Before she could reply, I did so.

I doubt if she had ever dealt with such an irate tourist before,
and she remained quite speechless.

The next day we said goodbye to all our friends and I decided
never to see any of them again. I was placing them in too much
danger. Things had not changed, the power of the KGB was still
absolute and my intrusion into their lives could only unsettle
them.

CHAPTER TWENTY-TWO

Our plane to Leningrad was stiflingly hot, and as we were the only foreigners on board we were objects of curiosity. We were only too pleased when we got out at the airport. For once the guide took us to the hotel advertised in the brochure.

The Leningrad Hotel is a vast modern hotel, such as can be found near airports all over the world. It was full of American tourists. The usual spy sat at a desk by the lifts and—a wonderful improvement—there was a bar on every floor serving drinks and sandwiches. As their opening times varied, there was always one available.

It was lunchtime. We took one look at the enormous dining-room of the hotel and decided to go into town instead for one last Russian meal.

Practically all the tables in the Sadko Restaurant were empty, but the waitress took no notice of us and carried on stacking plates. When she did come, she was morose and unsmiling and almost everything on the menu was 'off'. We had to settle for broth with *pirojki* followed by *blini* with salt herring. She brought it all together, and lukewarm, so I said something to her in Russian. She obviously wasn't interested in my criticism, until I took out some chewing-gum. She took it, and gave us her first smile. 'For my little boy,' she said. I then produced the inevitable sample of French perfume and suggested that she took it as a souvenir. Her whole attitude changed; her eyes shone, and she told us naïvely that it had always been her dream to possess French perfume.

'Would you like caviar with hot *blinis*?' she suggested.

She brought them and stood talking to us. It is quite extraordinary how warmly and generously Russians respond to friendliness. It is not simply that bribery works miracles, but also the fact that someone is interested enough to care.

We decided to have another tour of the town and hailed a taxi.

The driver was very jovial. We praised the beauty of the city and began a long conversation with him. Whatever we had in the West, he assured us they had it bigger and better. Although this was rather annoying, his pride and sense of patriotism—so often absent in the West—was rather endearing. He lived, he said, in Leningrad, with his wife and son, and he also had a summer cottage. 'In fact, I have a wonderful life. I have everything I want.'

'You are very nearly a millionaire, then?' I joked.

To my surprise he answered 'We have plenty of millionaires in Leningrad, and you can say I am one of them.'

'I thought there was no such thing under the communist régime,' I parried.

He laughed. 'Why not?'

I liked him in spite of his ridiculous bragging; at least there was no need to draw him out. He was quite outspoken, volunteering information, so in the end I took the plunge and said 'What's your government like? Do you approve of it, or are you like us, always grumbling whatever government you have?'

He was genuinely surprised. 'Why should I grumble? Things aren't quite as good as they were under Stalin, but it can't be helped. He was a father figure, a real *batka* [little father] to us, and how he loved us!'

For a moment I was taken aback; I had taken a liking to this man, and here he was praising the arch-assassin Stalin. The army officer had been right, there were still Stalinists left. This one did not attempt to hide his admiration, and later Tousia told me that from that moment the expression on my face changed. I don't doubt it. But I carried en with the conversation all the same.

'I thought Stalin was a Georgian, not a Russian?'

'So he was.'

'One of your Marxist-Leninist compatriots' (I didn't want to use Medvedeff's name) 'has written a biography of Stalin that is far from flattering. He cites so many executions of party men, it is quite frightening.'

'Stalin knew what he was doing. It was all for the safety of the country, and you can see how well we all live now because of him.'

He was perhaps the only communist I ever met on all my trips to Russia. As he dropped us off back at the hotel, I remembered another occasion when a young party member, the only one I had ever met, the son of a friend, returned to Russia after his first mission abroad. He was welcomed by all his family and friends, and by a profusion of *zakusi* and vodka. Everyone wanted to know what he thought of France, but he was very reticent, probably acting on instructions. Then one of his friends asked him 'What about communism there?'

A perplexed expression came over his face. 'Why should they want communism?' he asked.

In the hotel we ran into an American woman and her daughter whom we had talked to previously. 'We're off to the commission shop to buy antiques,' I said. 'Do you want to come with us?'

We all crowded into another taxi. The commission shop was full but not many people were buying. There were old clocks, bronzes, large malachite vases which would have taken two men to carry and other ill-assorted objects from another era. Many of them were damaged or had parts missing. I found a Sèvres statuette with only one arm; I put it down again and after a while the assistant found me another one, this time complete, for the same price.

As we foraged enthusiastically the Russian crowd watched us with great interest, until finally one of them asked us 'Are you going to buy those things?'

'Probably.'

'But where are you going to put them?'

'In our homes.' (Though I was conscious that they scarcely understood what we meant by 'homes'.)

'Will they let them out?'

'I hope so!' I didn't mention that we planned to smuggle them out.

We went on selecting and rejecting, while the crowd continued to stare at us. We had to work out how many roubles we had left, and how much space we had in our cases. The Americans were in raptures over some of their finds, and so were we.

Everything was either grossly underpriced or equally overpriced. Eventually I discovered that this was because of the way in which commission shops are run. A Russian who wishes to sell an old fridge, a television, a frying-pan, an antique or any such object is compelled by law to take it to these state-run shops which charge a ten per cent commission on all sales. They set the prices of objects by an extraordinarily arbitrary method, using a booklet which lists such simple categories as

Pair of shoes, old
Pair of shoes, new
Man's suit, large
Man's suit, small
Bronze, up to x centimetres
Bronze, more than x centimetres

The quality, condition, materials, and the current fashions are not allowed for in this bureaucratic system, and hence the extraordinary prices.

With our antique loot we returned to the hotel tired and thirsty. I went out to one of the bars to fetch some food and drinks to take to our room. There was a choice of the excellent Russian fruit juices. I chose the sandwiches and then asked the barmaid to pour out two glasses of these fruit juices.

'Where are they?' she asked.

'What do you mean?'

'The glasses.'

'I thought you would have them,' I replied.

'No, you must bring your own if you want to take drinks back to your room.'

'Look here,' I said, 'how do you expect tourists to have glasses?'

'There are tooth glasses in your bathrooms,' she explained kindly. 'You bring them and I'll fill them.' She was teaching me how to behave in a first-class hotel!

As I carried our tooth glasses back to our room, filled to the brim with fruit juice, I met our American friends.

'How on earth did you manage?' they exclaimed. Americans love to go native, and a few minutes later they joined us with their tooth glasses and a bottle of Russian champagne, the quality of which surprised me. It was very good and very dry. By the evening all the American contingent had cottoned on, and we were most amused to see them constantly going up and down the corridors with their tooth glasses.

The next morning we were told that there would be an excursion to Pushkino. The guide hoped we would join them, and I was about to agree, until she announced that it would have to be paid for in sterling. I had thought it was included in the price of the tour, and I had plenty of Russian currency I wanted to get rid of. Eventually we came to an arrangement; the guide was so keen for us to join the party that I wondered if two such stray sheep as Tousia and I would be a black mark against her. She certainly wanted us back in the fold.

Pushkino, of course, is the new name for Tsarskoye Selo. It was razed to the ground during the Leningrad blockade, and the restoration is a marvel of Russian skill and artistry. Perhaps they needed a war to bring home to them how much of their artistic and cultural tradition had suffered. Our guide took us through enfilades of salons that had been restored down to the last detail; the painted ceilings and the oil paintings were all there, and she explained that only the buildings had been destroyed. All the furnishings had been moved out before the German onslaught.

'Please observe the tapestries,' she announced. 'All the textiles here were woven at our largest factory, the Red Rose in Moscow.' How could she have suspected that Tousia and I were the granddaughters of its founder? But for his courage, tenacity and forethought they probably would not have it today. But she was young, and she had probably not been taught that most of the industrial expansion in her country between 1860 and the revolution had been the work of foreigners. Nor could she know of the deep affection those settlers had retained for the country that had thrown them out.

We had quite a job packing our things for the journey home. The worst problem was Mitia's pictures, which were too large for our cases. We had to wrap them up with brown paper and string provided by the hotel porter. In the Customs Hall a young man scrutinised our passports carefully. 'Aha,' he said, 'you were born in Russia. You must speak Russian?'

It was useless to deny it.

'Well, what kind of souvenirs have you got?'

'All kinds of souvenirs to take back to friends. You know how it is.' He did not, of course.

'Any caviar?'

'A small box only,' I lied. 'It is so difficult to obtain.'

He nodded in agreement. I hoped he would not discover the two kilos I had bought through Tania.

'Have you bought any antiques in the commission shops?'

'Yes, a figure of a Cossack saying goodbye to his girlfriend.'

'Where is it?'

'I haven't the slightest idea. It must be in one of the three cases. You will have to look for it.'

I hoped it would be too much trouble; luckily it was. Then he spotted the brown paper parcel. 'What is that?'

'Pictures of birch trees which an old Russian pensioner gave us to remind us of your country.'

This flattered him. 'How many are there? Two?'

'Yes, one for me and one for my sister.'

'Are they both the same, then?' he asked.

I nodded, much as I would have liked to point out that two identical paintings would be very *ne koultourno*!

'All right,' he grinned, and wished us a safe journey.

Long ago when going through some old papers I found a letter written in 1867 to my grandmother. It was from her husband, who was on his way from Russia to Paris. In those days rich merchants needed to be adventurous. There was unrest in Poland, and the journey was slow and fraught with dangers. The letter, written from somewhere en route, stated that as he had crossed the frontiers of Russia he had felt like a man taking off a very dirty shirt and putting on a clean one. How well I understood him now!

I had laid the ghost of the Russia of my childhood, Holy Russia, so human, impulsive and sentimental. It no longer existed, and the new Russia with its atheism and its total distrust permeating every level of society held no charms for me.

CHAPTER TWENTY-THREE

Four years were to pass before I returned to Russia, this time to look for antiques and to buy ikons from the Russian government.

'You ought to go there again,' a young friend told me. 'The country has changed a great deal in the last four or five years.' But in what way, he did not say.

One change, I knew, was that it was no longer possible to buy black-market roubles from various foreign embassies, but I was able to obtain forbidden roubles quite openly in London at six to one instead of the official 1.28 to the pound, although I was warned that it was illegal to take roubles into the Soviet Union.

My American friend and I booked with a British tour operator—I had had enough of Intourist by this time—but when we arrived in Moscow we launched out on our own. The driver of the first taxi we used refused to give us any change, nor would any other taxi-driver do so. And on the following morning my companion complained that he had not slept all night, and showed me itching lumps on his neck and arms. 'What do you suppose they are?' he asked.

I recognised them at once. 'Bed bugs,' I said. At first he refused to believe me.

'You are obviously receiving the full Russian treatment,' I said by way of consolation, and took him to the floor attendant. 'What's this?' I said, pointing to the bites.

'Oh dear!' she exclaimed apologetically. 'Bed bugs again. I'll have the gentleman's room fumigated at once.'

This happened at the Leningrad Hotel, one of the best hotels in the Soviet Union. While we were there I noticed that life for the ordinary tourist had become far more regimented, and that by the use of special hotels, special restaurants, and because of both the language barrier and Intourist officialdom, they had become almost completely segregated from meeting ordinary

Russians. We, on the other hand, were constantly being pro-
positioned in the street. 'Do you want to buy ikons?' 'Have you
any jeans?' 'Will you sell me your coat?'—the Russian appetite
for anything Western had now become almost insatiable. And
yet supplies of goods in the Russian shops were better than before,
and nobody starved, but the food was monotonous, unappetising
and expensive. Even when paying in black-market roubles the
prices were as high as anywhere in the West. The list of quite
ordinary goods that were unobtainable was still very long, but
the Russians were now beginning to discover that these things
were available elsewhere. And so Western goods had become the
new currency which was used in the ever increasing bribery and
fiddling.

'How else could we subsist on our meagre wages?' was the
universal excuse. Because I could explain what I wanted and was
nevertheless a stranger in their midst, my companion and I were
welcome everywhere, and I make no apology for exploiting the
Russian craving for what we had. We could enter any restaurant
while a queue of hopefuls was refused admission; an Intourist
taxi would willingly take us wherever we wanted to go, and I was
able to wangle all sorts of other facilities—all for jeans, tights and
chewing-gum.

One day we were accosted in a Moscow street by a man offering
to sell us antiques. His name was Kolia, and he told us he was a
dentist by profession. His room in a communal apartment was
full of ikons, silver items, *objets d'art* and even Fabergé eggs. He
was constantly at our beck and call during the four days we were
in Moscow, and in the end I asked him if he ever went to work.

He seemed surprised. 'I go to my office once a month,' he
said.

'Why aren't you reported to the authorities?'

'I go to collect my monthly pay—two hundred and twenty-five
roubles—and I turn it straight over to my superior. In return he
stamps my cards, to prove to the authorities that I attend regularly and am a good worker.'

'And that's how you manage to be able to deal in antiques?'

'Of course,' Kolia replied. 'How else do you expect me to live
with a wife who loves pretty things when I'm paid such a pittance?'

'Are you an exception?' I asked.

'Good Lord, no! Most of my friends do the same.'

A similar story was told to me by a young taxi-driver. He had had such an old car that it was constantly breaking down, and he had got a better one by giving his boss a bottle of whisky every month. 'I'm not complaining,' he said. 'It's well worth it. Besides, here everyone fiddles.'

In a Leningrad bookshop I struck up a conversation with a young man of about twenty-three. He was the son of a general, an excellent linguist and he had a very good job. He invited us to the two large rooms where he lived with his wife. The couple were well off by Soviet standards, yet they asked us if we could get them a feeding-bottle for the baby they were expecting. When they were driving us out to their *dacha* in their car, the young husband suddenly confided that he was a party member.

'Not that I wanted to join,' he explained, 'but you must understand that if I hadn't it would have been the end of the road.' I just nodded. He had obtained a special concession from the authorities allowing his wife not to work during her pregnancy. 'Maybe some day I shall be able to free her from all obligation to work. After all, she doesn't need to work.'

'You don't really approve of the régime?' I asked.

'I don't have to. Even a party member can be a dissident,' he replied.

'But under Stalin this would have been different?'

'Yes, of course, but Stalin is no longer.'

His wife would have dearly liked to see the West. I comforted her, saying that she would one day, as she was so young and things were bound to change. 'Have no illusions,' her husband interrupted, and he told me a current Russian joke:

Brezhnev and Kosygin were discussing lifting the travel restrictions.

'No,' said Brezhnev, 'we can't relax the rules. If we do, you and I will be the only people left in the country.'

'No, Lenia,' Kosygin replied, 'you are mistaken. There will only be you.'

'But Brezhnev is old,' I said. 'Surely it will be different when he goes?'

'After him it will be Romanoff,' the young man replied, 'and he is very tough.'

What an unfortunate name for a future ruler of the Russian proletariat, I reflected.

'We Russians know full well how arrogant our rulers are,' he went on. 'They live in such secrecy that we can only guess at the extent of their privileges. We know that they live in special blocks, shop in special shops and never use public transport. We accept that as we did the autocracy of the tsars. The ordinary citizen has not really changed much. He is still a simple fellow at heart, still gets drunk, and in a country where religion has been abolished he still believes more in God than in communism.'